Holywell St

Maltby's
the
Bookbinders

1926

New
College

New College Lane

Cattle St

Hertford
College

King Edward St

Merton St.

OXFORD, 1922-1926

Hall Brothers

THE NAG'S
HEAD
7 MILES

Oxford

Evelyn Waugh's Oxford

Evelyn Waugh's Oxford
1922–1966

BARBARA COOKE

With illustrations by Amy Dodd

Bodleian Library
UNIVERSITY OF OXFORD

For David Bradshaw
'Friend, colleague, force of nature'

First published in 2018 by the Bodleian Library
Broad Street, Oxford OX1 3BG
www.bodleianshop.co.uk

ISBN 978 1 85124 487 4

Foreword © Alexander Waugh, 2018
Text © Barbara Cooke, 2018

Archival materials
© 2018, The Evelyn Waugh Estate. All rights reserved.

Illustrations on endpapers and pp. 77–140 © Amy Dodd, 2018

All other images, unless specified on p. 171, © Bodleian Library, University of Oxford, 2018.

Barbara Cooke has asserted her right to be identified as the author of this Work.

Extracts from Evelyn Waugh's letters and manuscripts
are reproduced by kind permission of The Evelyn Waugh Estate.

Extract from the correspondence of A.H. Trelawny Ross
is reproduced by kind permission of Carol Trelawny Ross.

Extracts from A.L. Rowse's annotated copy of *Brideshead Revisted*
are reproduced by kind permission of The Royal Institution of Cornwall.

Every effort has been made to trace copyright holders and to obtain permission for the use of copyright material; any errors or omissions will be incorporated in future editions of this book.

Cover design by Dot Little at the Bodleian Library
Designed and typeset in 12½ on 16 Perpetua by illuminati, Grosmont
Printed and bound in China by C&C Offset Printing Co. Ltd
on 120 gsm IKPP woodfree paper

British Library Catalogue in Publishing Data
A CIP record of this publication is available from the British Library

Contents

ACKNOWLEDGEMENTS   vii

FOREWORD   *Alexander Waugh*   viii

PREFACE   xii

EVELYN WAUGH'S LIFE & WORKS   xiv

Evelyn Arthur St John Waugh, 1903–1966   I

EVELYN WAUGH'S CITY

City of Invention   27

City of Memory   46

City of Imagination   63

EXPLORING WAUGH'S OXFORD

Hertford College   78

The New Theatre   81

Hall Brothers   85

New College   88

The Hypocrites Club   92

Balliol College   96
The Junk Shop   100
The Oxford Canal   103
Alice's Shop   107
The Oxford Union   110
St John's College & Campion Hall   114
Maltby's the Bookbinders   118
Pubs   121
The Railway Station   127
The Old Palace   130
Christ Church   133
Oxford Botanic Garden   136
Merton Street   140

NOTES   143
BIBLIOGRAPHY   162
IMAGE CREDITS   171
INDEX   172

Acknowledgements

First thanks must go to the splendid archivists who have given so freely of their time and knowledge during the writing of this book: to Oxford's college archivists Judith Curthoys (Christ Church), Lucy Rutherford (Hertford) and Jeffrey Hackney (Wadham), to Rick Watson, Eric Colleary, Pat Fox and all at the Harry Ransom Center, to Mark Everett and to all those private collectors who prefer to keep off-radar. I am exceptionally grateful to Alexander Waugh for all the same reasons, to which must be added his warmth, hospitality and unfailing camaraderie.

Thank you to Chris at Bike Zone Oxford, for discussing the history of his shop. This project would have been much harder without the works of friends and colleagues around the world to draw on, especially those of Martin Stannard, Selina Hastings, Donat Gallagher, Naomi Milthorpe, Douglas Lane Patey, Paula Byrne and the greatly missed John Howard Wilson. Thank you to everyone who read and commented on parts of this book in draft: Helen Hillsdon, Helen Hildebrand, Jon Edwards, Elizabeth Corbishley, Nonia William Korteling, Carina Hart and, most importantly, Tom O'Hare. He knows how rarely teachers get the credit they deserve, and so I'd like to end by celebrating Juliette Ledsham and Louise Hindle for pushing hard when it mattered most. I hope they like the result.

Foreword

ALEXANDER WAUGH

Since 1981, when Granada Television's lavish eleven-episode adaptation of *Brideshead Revisited* was first screened around the world, the city of Oxford has often been defined, in the popular imagination, as the Arcadian Oxford of Evelyn Waugh's imagination. Today's English or American tourist strolling on a balmy day down The Broad, passing by the old Bodleian, the Sheldonian Theatre or through the hallowed sandstone cloisters of numerous old colleges, cannot fail to be reminded of the distinctive, fruity voice-over of Jeremy Irons, extolling the beauty of Oxford in rich, mellifluous phrases. *Brideshead* is a book about a great house, reduced in time of war to a military barracks, at which one stationed officer, Charles Ryder, speaking in the first person, nostalgically recalls his past association with the house and its family. Waugh wrote it as a serving officer in 1944. He was filled with creative energy and enthusiasm for his work. It was to be his 'magnum opus'.[1] In 1960 he recalled his work on the novel during a 'bleak period of privation and threatening disaster – the period of soya beans and Basic English'. Its composition he remembered as a 'kind of gluttony ... for the splendours of the recent past, and for rhetorical and ornamental language, which now with a full stomach I find distasteful'.[2]

This gluttony for the recent past and of rhetorical and ornamental language may well have been provoked by Waugh's sense of wartime privation in 1944, but it was also the result of a hereditary tic. *Brideshead* was conceived shortly after the death of Waugh's father. Arthur Waugh (1867–1943), publisher, author and very minor poet, entertained a lifelong, obsessive and fatuous nostalgia for the gentle sandstone architecture of Sherborne in Dorset, where he had been schooled. Scarcely a day would pass in which he would not rhapsodize on the subject of Sherborne, the old school which he felt bound him in some peculiar and spiritual way to his older son, Alec. Had Alec not disgraced himself at Sherborne School by kissing a younger boy called Davis Minor, his brother Evelyn would surely have been sent there too. The daily 'rhetorical and ornamental' expression which Arthur used to describe the town of Sherborne fell below the prose standards later set of his younger son:

> In the summer term [Arthur wrote in *Country Life* in 1916], when the Abbey chimes sound more than commonly mellow and serene, when the meadows round the Yeo are full of king-cups, and the soft air of the west can scarcely stir the lime trees in the Courts, there is perhaps some temptation to take life easily at Sherborne.[3]

Waugh was an officer in the Special Services Brigade, billeted at an army base in Sherborne, when he heard of his father's death. Two months later he wrote in his dairy 'I am so bored with everything military' that 'I don't want to be of service to anyone or anything. I simply want to do my work as an artist.'[4] And so he began *Brideshead Revisited*. If, in that brief interregnum of mourning, he had taken the time to reread his father's autobiography, he would have reminded himself of the following reminiscence of Oxford in wartime:

> Oxford, who has welcomed so many armies home, now victorious, now again vanquished, but all alike her sons, Oxford seems

to have suffered more than most institutions from the brief but
biting ordeal of war. I remember standing in Tom Quad at Christ
Church, midway in the first year of hostilities, and wondering if
the place could ever be the same again as it was when we were
young. Everything for which Oxford stood was at a standstill; the
Colleges were barracks, the meadows drill yards; the long tradition
of manners which 'makyth man' was broken.[5]

And how similar is this in style and thought to Waugh's most celebrated
description of Oxford in *Brideshead Revisited*?

Oxford – submerged now and obliterated, irrecoverable as Lyon-
nesse, so quickly have the waters come flooding in – Oxford, in
those days, was still a city of aquatint. In her spacious and quiet
streets men walked and spoke as they had done in Newman's day;
her autumnal mists, her grey springtime, and the rare glory of her
summer days – such as that day – when the chestnut was in flower
and the bells rang out high and clear over her gables and cupolas
exhaled the soft airs of centuries of youth.[6]

While Waugh's nostalgia for Oxford in *Brideshead* informs the modern
tourist's dreamy love of this city, it was not how Waugh always saw the
place. In 1930 he demanded a 'small expenditure on dynamite to rid us
forever of the clock tower at Carfax, the Town Hall, the Indian Institute,
the High Street front of Oriel, the Holywell front of New College and
the whole of Hertford, thus changing Oxford from a comparatively ugly
city to a comparatively beautiful one'.[7] Four months after writing this
he was extolling Oxford as 'a city of peculiar grace and magnificence
… in which it is convenient to segregate a certain number of the young
of the nation while they are growing up'.[8] Towards the end of his life
his interest in the city was limited to her Roman Catholic life, which
centred, for him, around Fr Martin D'Arcy's Campion Hall and Mgr
Ronald Knox's Trinity College.

As an undergraduate Waugh spent much of his time drinking, social-izing, spending too much money and what he called 'eating wild honey in the wilderness'[9] but, like his character Charles Ryder, he never looked back in regret:

> 'I'm Sorry Jasper,' I said. 'I know it must be embarrassing for you, but I happen to *like* this bad set. I *like* getting drunk at luncheon, and though I haven't yet spent quite double my allowance, I undoubtedly shall before the end of term. I usually have a glass of champagne about this time. Will you join me?'[10]

Waugh's Oxford career began in a blaze of glory. A school friend noted in his diary of 15 December 1921:

> A really excellent day. It started off at breakfast with the news that Evelyn got a £100 a year scholarship at Hertford for 5 years... He is awfully bucked and makes no attempt to hide it.[11]

Three years later Waugh's Oxford undergraduate career, reading Modern History with a tutor he hated, ended in ignominy. He left the University with no money, insurmountable debts and no degree. But the Waughs have never done well at Oxford. Evelyn's father obtained a poor third at New College; of his three sons two were awarded third-class degrees, while his eldest, Auberon, was expelled from Christ Church for failing his prelims in his first year and his nephew, Peter Waugh, left Lincoln College with no degree. I surpassed them all by failing even to get a place at the University.

Barbara Cooke, a leading expert on Waugh's life and work, offers an engaging account of Oxford's effect on Waugh and Waugh's effect on Oxford that should leave the reader with a refreshed, if slightly altered, view of both.

Preface

In *Brideshead Revisited*, Evelyn Waugh's most famous novel, he describes Oxford in the 1920s as a 'city of aquatint'. It's an image that encapsulates the story's nostalgia for a recent, idealized past. But it does not tell the full story of Evelyn Waugh's Oxford, the place he inhabited, literally, during his student years and, artistically, for the rest of his life. Waugh's published career begins and ends in this city.

At university Waugh was dazzled by a glamorous world totally unlike anything he had known before. It fired his creative impulses and engendered a rich legacy of comic, lyrical and unforgettable works. This book explores both that creative process and its legacy in the context of Waugh's life. It begins by looking at the graphic art, journalism and short stories Waugh produced at Oxford before taking a longer view of the city's depiction through his first and last published works, 'The Balance', *Decline and Fall*, *Brideshead Revisited* and *A Little Learning*. Romantic melancholy is much in evidence here, but it is only one shade in a complex textual palette that also features wit, absurdity and pert social commentary.

The second half of the book meanders through Oxford itself, stopping at locations which tell their own stories within the grander narrative of Waugh's life and works. Each can be read individually; together they contribute to a wider understanding of Waugh's relationships with family, friends and enemies, his self-perception and self-representation, and his attitude to the material and spiritual worlds. These discussions have their physical roots in Oxford and their conceptual roots in Waugh's texts.

No prior experience of either Evelyn Waugh or the city of Oxford is necessary to navigate this book. It opens with a timeline and brief biography, and every location visited can be found on the map which lies at either end.

Evelyn Waugh's Life & Works

1885–89   Evelyn Waugh's father Arthur attends New College, Oxford, and leaves with a double third in Mods and Greats

8 July 1898   Waugh's brother Alec is born

28 October 1903   Evelyn Arthur St John, son of Arthur and Catherine Waugh, is born at 11 Hillfield Road, West Hampstead

10 September 1911   Waugh writes and illustrates his first diary entry: 'My History'

May 1917   Waugh attends Lancing College in the South Downs

July 1917   Alec Waugh's *The Loom of Youth* is published

11 September 1921   Arthur and Evelyn Waugh visit New College, Oxford, Arthur's alma mater

14 December 1921   Hertford College tutor C.R.M.F. Cruttwell writes to congratulate Waugh on his history scholarship: 'the quality of your English style [was] about the best of any of the candidates'

January 1922   Waugh goes up to Hertford College, Oxford

8 February 1922   Waugh makes his maiden speech at the Oxford Union

Autumn 1922   Alastair Graham goes up to Brasenose College, Oxford

December 1922   Tom Driberg visits Waugh in Oxford and is taken to the Hypocrites Club

April 1923   The first issue of *The Oxford Broom* appears, featuring Waugh's cover design

Catherine and Arthur Waugh with Alec and Evelyn (*left*) at Arthur's childhood home, 1904.

May 1923	'Portrait of Young Man With Career' is published in the *Isis*
June 1923	*The Oxford Broom* publishes 'Anthony, Who Sought Things That Were Lost'
23–28 June 1923	OUDS perform *The Rhesus*, for which Waugh has designed the programme cover
August 1923	'Edward of Unique Achievement' is published in *Cherwell*
Autumn 1923	Alastair Graham fails his preliminary exams and is sent down
28 November 1923	First outing of the Railway Club
December 1923	Alastair Graham stays at Underhill for the first time
29 July 1924	Waugh is awarded a third in his viva, and leaves Oxford before completing the nine terms of residence required to claim his degree
31 October 1925	Waugh breaks his ankle crawling out of a window in an Oxford bar and spends his recuperation reading up on the Pre-Raphaelites

October 1926	'The Balance' published in *Georgian Stories, 1926*
April 1928	*Rossetti* is published
27 June 1928	Waugh marries Evelyn Florence Margaret Winifred Gardner in a very small ceremony
September 1928	*Decline and Fall* is published
July 1929	Evelyn Gardner leaves Waugh for John Heygate
January 1930	*Vile Bodies* is published
September 1930	*Labels* is published
29 September 1930	Waugh is received into the Roman Catholic Church
October 1930	Waugh travels to Abyssinia as a *Times* reporter
November 1931	*Remote People* is published
October 1932	*Black Mischief* is published
September 1933	Waugh meets Laura Laetitia Gwendolen Evelyn Herbert, thirteen years his junior
March 1934	*Ninety-Two Days* is published
July–August 1934	Waugh goes on an Arctic expedition with Hugh Lygon and the explorer Alexander Glen
September 1934	*A Handful of Dust* is published
September 1935	*Edmund Campion: Jesuit and Martyr* is published
July 1936	*Mr Loveday's Little Outing and Other Sad Stories* is published
October 1936	*Waugh in Abyssinia* is published
17 April 1937	Waugh marries Laura Herbert; they go on to have seven children
May 1938	*Scoop!* is published
June 1939	*Robbery Under Law* (US title *Mexico: An Object Lesson*) is published
December 1939	Waugh joins the Royal Marines
March 1942	*Put Out More Flags* is published
December 1942	*Work Suspended: Two Chapters of an Unfinished Novel* is published
June 1943	Arthur Waugh dies

May 1945   *Brideshead Revisited* is published

3 September 1945   Waugh revisits Hertford College and is presented with the collected works of Shakespeare that Terence Greenidge stole from him twenty years before

December 1947   *Scott-King's Modern Europe* is published

5 May 1948   Waugh addresses the Tyndale Society, Hertford's debating club, on the subject of his Knox biography; he remarks that he never expected to be welcomed back so warmly

October 1950   *Helena* is published

September 1952   *Men at Arms* is published

May 1953   *Love Among the Ruins* is published

June 1953   *The Loved One* is published

6 December 1954   Catherine Waugh dies

July 1955   *Officers and Gentlemen* is published

July 1957   *The Ordeal of Gilbert Pinfold* is published

October 1959   *The Life of Right Reverend Ronald Knox* is published

September 1960   *A Tourist in Africa* is published

October 1961   *Unconditional Surrender* (US title *The End of the Battle*) is published

October 1963   *Basil Seal Rides Again* is published

14 November 1963   Railway Club anniversary dinner

September 1964   *A Little Learning* is published

10 April 1966   Waugh dies at home, on Easter Sunday

Evelyn Arthur St John Waugh, 1903–1966

CHILDHOOD

Evelyn Arthur St John Waugh was born on 28 October 1903 at 11 Hillfield Road, West Hampstead. When he was about four the family moved to Underhill, a house built and named by his father Arthur, in nearby North End Road.[1] Evelyn's own name was his mother Catherine's choice. Its frivolity immediately set him apart from his older brother, the more conventionally named Alec, and would lead to confusion and embarrassment throughout his life. Anyone from a *Times* literary critic to an Italian army officer was liable to assume its possessor was a girl,[2] and Alec, inspired by school friends who thought his little brother must be neuter, called him 'It'.[3]

Evelyn's second name was also a source of difficulty, it being one of the only things he had in common with his father. Arthur Waugh, managing director of the publisher Chapman & Hall, was jolly, fond of home life and – according to Evelyn at least – very comfortable to be middle-of-the-road. By contrast, his younger son was caustic, perfectionist from an early age and destined to spend large chunks of time avoiding his family. Arthur got on better with Alec, who fully returned his love. One holiday

OPPOSITE Evelyn Waugh with his nanny Lucy Hodges, c. 1906.

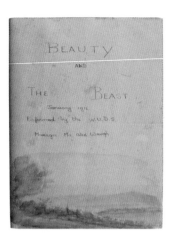

RIGHT Theatre programme for *Beauty and the Beast*, produced at Underhill in January 1912.

FAR RIGHT *The Pistol Troop Magazine*, 1912, produced by Evelyn and his friends and bound by Arthur Waugh. This frontispiece was also designed by Evelyn.

when Alec returned from his prep school, Fernden, Arthur covered the face of their grandfather clock with a poster reading: 'Welcome home to the Heir of Underhill'.[4] Evelyn fully grasped the significance of the act. Shut out from Arthur and Alec's dyadic relationship of mutual admiration, Evelyn relied instead on the love of his mother and his nurse, a devout young Methodist called Lucy Hodges.

Evelyn attended nonconformist services with Lucy, while the Waugh parents had more High Church leanings. Arthur Waugh in particular preferred a touch of theatre in his Sunday service, and for a time attended the performances of a 'totally preposterous parson' who liked to illustrate Matthew 5:13 by pouring salt onto the church carpet.[5] Nearby, Evelyn's maiden aunts ran Sunday-school classes from the old family home at Midsomer Norton. He soaked up these rival religious influences with more enjoyment than discrimination.

Evelyn stayed longer in the domestic circle than most boys of his time and class, for instead of following Alec to Fernden (where the latter had once been made to eat his own sick)[6] he attended a local day school, Heath Mount. It was at this point, Waugh later reflected, that he really

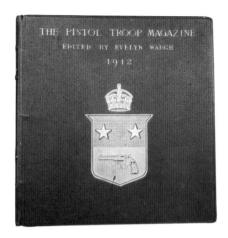

began to know his father. Alec was away boarding, and every morning Arthur would walk Evelyn across Hampstead Heath to school. On the way, he conjured up vivid pictures for his 'audience of one' of the 'highwaymen, rebels, defaulting financiers [and] the poets and painters who lived in the district', interweaving their true stories with 'certain wholly fabulous creatures'.[7] These morning walks were just one facet of the rich imaginative world Arthur created for his sons. Together, they also formed their own theatre company and performed at Underhill alongside their neighbours Jean and Phillipa (Philla) Fleming. Their handmade programmes were decorated with pressed flowers, watercolours by local friends and photographs of the cast.[8] When Evelyn began producing his own writing, which he did around the age of seven, it was treated with the same care: his juvenilia were diligently preserved and, sometimes, specially bound by Arthur's publishing friends.[9]

After dinner the Waugh family would gather in Arthur's library (or 'book-room', as he preferred to call it) and listen as he read from his favourite writers Kipling, Keats and Shakespeare. Evelyn's response to these readings changed according to the wider circumstances of his life.

The Pistol Troop, *c.* 1910. Waugh is second from right.

As a child, he marvelled at his father's rich tones and dramatic manner. During the First World War, when Alec was training at Sandhurst, they filled the last precious minutes of his weekend leave; years later, English lyric poets still evoked for Waugh not 'feverish eyes and wispy beards over the absinthe of the Café Royal but … puttees, heavy boots and a sturdy young soldier with a cup of cocoa under the rosy lights of the book-room at home'.[10] As a raw divorcee forced back by penury to Underhill, Evelyn grew to hate his father's performances as the soundtrack to his incarceration.[11] Arthur's library, however, was the bedrock of Waugh's literary education: by the time he was thirteen, when other boys were occupied with *Chums* and *The Boy's Friend*, he was reading Malory's *Morte D'Arthur* and Compton Mackenzie's *Sinister Street*.[12] School provision could not compare.

Waugh (*top left*) as a sixth former at Lancing College, 1921.

In volume 2 of *Sinister Street* its hero, Michael Fane, starts life at Oxford University.[13] Evelyn was reading about Michael's adventures as he negotiated the bleak reality of an English boarding school in wartime. He was first sent to Lancing College, a flinty ecclesiastical establishment in the South Downs, in May 1917. Arthur had chosen the school based on his son's apparent enthusiasm for Christianity; Evelyn had recently gone through a phase of creating shrines in his bedroom and tried his mother's patience with increasingly elaborate night-time prayers.[14] All this, however, was over by the time he arrived at boarding school and before he left he had declared himself an atheist.[15] He would not rediscover religion for another ten years.

Food rationing and compulsory military training conspired to make the already austere regime at Lancing positively miserable. Again, his

separateness from his father and brother was marked: they had both gone
to Sherborne, but Alec's behaviour during and immediately after his
schooling had prevented Evelyn from doing the same.[16] Earlier that year
Alec had published his first novel. Entitled *The Loom of Youth*, it was set in
a thinly disguised Sherborne where brutal punishments were meted out to
the boarders, and young boys became blushingly fond of one another. It is
difficult now to see what had been so scandalous about the *Loom*. Passages
such as '[h]e did not know what his real sentiments were; he did not even
attempt to analyse them. He only knew that when he was with Morcombe
he was indescribably happy'[17] seem so mild that it is hard to believe they
could ever have caused moral outrage. Nevertheless, Sherborne was
incensed by its depiction in the novel[18] and Evelyn's attendance was out
of the question.

Instead, Waugh forged his own path at Lancing. It was a lonely
existence. Despite rising to positions of responsibility such as the editor-
ship of the *Lancing College Magazine* (*LCM*), Waugh always felt isolated at
school and in his last term confided in his diary: 'No one here seems to
have any real friends ... I wonder ... how much friendship is created
by memory – a good deal, I should imagine.'[19] Instead of 'real friends'
Waugh had 'cronies'; boys like Hugh Molson and Roger Fulford who
helped to set up and run school debating society,[20] and an early admirer
named Dudley Carew with whom Waugh founded the Corpse Club 'for
people who are bored stiff'.[21] The club promoted total apathy towards
all things, and its animating spirit of disillusionment is also present in
Waugh's final editorial for the *LCM*:

> What will the young men of 1922 be?
>   ... It is a queer world which the old men have left them and
> they will have few ideals and illusions to console them when they
> 'get to feeling old'. They will not be a happy generation.[22]

S.W.R.D. Bandaranaike (*top row, third from right*) during his term as secretary of the Oxford Union, 1923. Waugh's lover Richard Pares is top left.

This unhappiness contrasted sharply with the delight Waugh was soon to experience on a trip away from Lancing. He'd applied for a scholarship at Hertford, and in the second week of December 1921 travelled up to Oxford with Molson, who was trying for New College, to sit his exams. He 'simply loved' the general paper, and had a good stab at English, History and French. But the real joy was the social life on offer. When not in the Examination Schools, Waugh and Molson were warmly hosted by a succession of Lancing old boys. They went to the Union, where Waugh was impressed by S.W.R.D. Bandaranaike but disappointed with the overall quality of the debate, and to a play at the New Theatre. Neither boy wanted to leave. 'I think', Waugh wrote, 'that this last week has been one of the happiest I have ever known.'[23] Waugh agonized over the result of his exams, but he needn't have worried. On Thursday, 15 December he discovered that he'd won the Hertford scholarship,[24] and prepared to go up to university in the New Year.

OXFORD AND THE 1920S

Waugh matriculated in January 1922. He would spend just two and a half years as an undergraduate, but the experience was to have a lasting impact on his life and writing. In his last months at school Waugh had questioned how much he really wanted to go to university,[25] but the 'pure euphoria'[26] of his scholarship week had won over his doubt. He expected his student years to be transformative, and they were.

At first, Waugh stuck mostly to his college. He dined in hall, lunched in his rooms and socialized with Philip Machin, whom he'd known at Lancing. He also made his first new friend: Terence Greenidge, amateur film-maker and kleptomaniac. It wasn't long, however, before his studies went awry. Waugh had chosen to specialize in Representative Government, plucking the topic out of the air.[27] He soon realized it was a mistake, but instead of trying to change it he simply ignored work as much as he could. This infuriated Waugh's history tutor, C.R.M.F. Cruttwell, and sowed the seed of the two men's mutual and enduring loathing.

No diary survives from Waugh's university years. He says he was having too much fun to keep one;[28] others think he destroyed it.[29] Either way, there are few reliable dates for this period of Waugh's life, and when he came to write his autobiography forty years later his memory was flawed. In *A Little Learning* (1964) the impression Waugh gives of Oxford is of a permanent, joyful alcoholic haze punctuated by practical jokes, ineffectual speeches at the Union and contributions to student magazines. This was not the whole story, but Waugh's statement that he was 'reborn in full youth' at university is perfectly true. Freed from the different but equally stifling restrictions of school and home, he began to form a new identity for himself: elfin and dapper, cheerful and talkative.[30] He took to walking with a cane.

According to his contemporary Peter Quennell, at Oxford Waugh 'was a carefree and good-natured character, with an exuberant sense of fun and taste for human absurdities, but no trace of underlying bitterness'.[31]

Terence Greenidge soon introduced Waugh to the Hypocrites Club in St Aldate's, described by Waugh's cousin Claud Cockburn as a 'noisy, alcohol-soaked rat-warren by the river.'[32] Fellow history scholar A.L. Rowse added that it stank.[33] Many of the Hypocrites were Old Etonians, including Harold Acton; many, like Tom Driberg, were homosexual; nearly all of them were drunks. One Hypocrite, Richard Pares, belonged only to the second category. He had, Waugh remembered, 'an appealing pale face', a 'mop of fair hair' and 'blank blue eyes'.[34] In this homosocial community, almost as exclusively male as Lancing,[35] Waugh fell in love for the first time. The feeling was returned. Waugh designed a beautiful book plate for Pares featuring a swan and a rising sun, and Pares wrote him witty, complex love letters.[36]

But it was not to be. Pares, like Rowse, was a serious history student. Soon he was coaxed away from Waugh and the Hypocrites by 'Sligger' Urquhart, the dean of Balliol.[37] Waugh, loyal in love and hate alike, took every opportunity to make Urquhart suffer for his loss. He slandered him loudly and even impersonated him in a rare film performance, where he transferred some of his own sexual desires onto the hapless dean.[38]

Waugh did not follow Pares's example and return to his books. Instead he fell in love again, and this time the affair would last well beyond Oxford. It possibly overlapped with Waugh's first marriage too.[39] His new lover was Alastair Graham, a dreamy, upper-middle-class boy from Warwickshire. For most of their second year at Oxford, Graham and Waugh retreated into their own company.[40] Their seclusion was a foreshadowing of Graham's own later, solitary retreat from the world.[41]

Wrapped up in each other, neither boy did enough work for a decent degree. Graham failed his exams and was sent down.[42] Waugh got a third, but needed to be resident in Oxford for nine terms in order to claim it. Because he had gone up in a January, this meant staying on for a whole term after his final exams. By now, his extravagant lifestyle and taste for expensive books had drawn him deep into debt. Arthur Waugh had also got a third at Oxford, so tempered his criticism. Nevertheless, he was disappointed and refused to bankroll his profligate son any further. Waugh was left with no choice but to go down, without graduating, in the summer of 1924.[43]

During the six years following Waugh's departure from Oxford he would fall in love again (at least twice), marry and divorce. He would also publish three books. It was a hectic period characterized by passion, despair and feverish hard work, but it began in apathy. After a few abortive attempts to train in the applied arts – first as a draughtsman, then a cabinetmaker, and finally as apprentice to a printmaker – Waugh was forced to take a job as a master in a remote Welsh public school. It was the only career open to a man of his superior education and woefully inferior qualifications.[44] Although he was very unhappy, lonely, frustrated and still drinking too much, Waugh's purgatory in second-rate English preparatory schools served the useful function of providing him with raw comedic material for his first novel, *Decline and Fall* (1928).[45] Another arbitrary twist of fate led to the production of his first biography. In 1925, he'd broken an ankle crawling out of the window of an Oxford bar ('I was behaving very oddly, I think'). During his recovery he researched the Pre-Raphaelites in Arthur's book-room[46] and the following year wrote a pamphlet about the movement (*P.R.B.: An Essay on the Pre-Raphaelite Brotherhood, 1847–1854*). Anthony Powell, an Oxford acquaintance, later to find fame as the author of *Dance to the Music of Time*, was then working at Duckworth publishers. He read the pamphlet and passed it to his superiors, who commissioned Waugh to write *Rossetti: His Life and Works* (1928).[47]

Waugh's success was driven by ambition and the desire to surpass his father's comparatively 'humdrum'[48] achievements. However, this was not his only motivation. At the relatively young age of twenty-five, he was determined to get married. His fiancée was not the first woman with whom he'd fallen in love; before getting engaged, he'd been obsessed with an alcoholic and emotionally intense young girl called Olivia Plunket Greene. But Olivia rejected him,[49] and on 7 April 1927 Waugh recorded in his diary that he had met 'such a nice girl called Evelyn Gardner'.[50] Eight months later he proposed and, after a good deal of agonising,

Evelyns Waugh and Gardner at the Graham family home, May 1928.

'She-Evelyn' (as she was to become known) accepted him.[51] But there was a problem. She-Evelyn was from an aristocratic family who would not countenance her marrying an impoverished schoolmaster. So, Waugh turned to writing as a way of generating enough income to keep a wife.[52] This pragmatic approach to work would remain a distinguishing feature of Waugh's career. Writing might be a calling, but it was also a job.

The Evelyns married on 27 June 1928, but after just a year Waugh's wife left him. He was halfway through writing his second novel *Vile Bodies* at the time, and the 'defection'[53] plunged him into a deep depression which, he later said, fundamentally affected the tone of a book that begins in 'gaiety' but ends in global and personal disaster.[54] It was published in January 1930 to great acclaim, and consolidated Waugh's reputation as a talented satirical writer. In late September the same year, Waugh was received into the Roman Catholic Church.[55] Many of Waugh's Oxford friends, including Alfred Duggan, Hugh Lygon and Harold Acton, had either been brought up or were Catholic, and he had attended Masses with Alastair Graham.[56] While some of these men were in flight from their childhood religion, for Waugh Catholicism had come to represent a refuge from a world that had shown itself to be chaotic and decadent, and connected him to a tradition dating back two thousand years. His new faith became the centre of his life.

TRAVEL AND MARRIAGE

The early 1930s were years of drift for Waugh. He visited prostitutes, embarked upon a series of love affairs, and became infatuated with fellow Catholic Teresa (Baby) Jungman. Baby would never marry Waugh; even if she'd wanted to, in her eyes Evelyn Gardner would always be his true wife. But if she wasn't in love with Waugh, she was fond of him. Between 1930 and 1935 Waugh sent 'Sweet Tess'[57] more than seventy-five

love letters, which she kept secret until just before her death at the age
of 102.[58]

Waugh published five volumes of travel writing during the 1930s,
drawn from numerous trips undertaken more to escape England than
for any love of adventure for its own sake. Here, Waugh was moving
in on his brother's territory; Alec had developed a serious wanderlust
and already published several travelogues. Between them, Evelyn and
Alec carved up the globe: only the elder brother would write about 'the
Polynesian Islands, North America and the West Indies', leaving 'the
whole of Africa and a good slice of Asia' to the younger.[59] In a flush of
post-conversion enthusiasm for all things Italian, Waugh also covered
the invasion of Abyssinia (now Ethiopia) for the *Daily Mail*, one of a very

A troubled Waugh travelled extensively during the 1930s.

Evelyn and Laura Waugh on their wedding day, 17 April 1937.

few English newspapers to take a pro-Mussolini stance in the conflict. In 1934 he published *A Handful of Dust*, a bitter and latterly fantastic novel drawing on the now-tarnished world of the Bright Young People as well as his adventures in South America. It is now widely considered to be Waugh's most accomplished pre-World War II work, if not his finest novel.

In 1936 Waugh's first marriage was annulled. A year later, he married the twenty-year-old Laura Herbert. Laura was a Catholic aristocrat (and a cousin of his first wife), and her family was horrified by the prospect of her marrying a much older, middle-class divorcee. Laura's mother Mary and her sisters Gabriel and Bridget were eventually won over, and her grandmother Evelyn, Lady de Vesci bought the couple Piers Court in Gloucestershire as a wedding gift. Waugh could never get on with Laura's brother Auberon, however, who gave his sister away but spent the morning of the wedding begging her to change her mind.[60]

Laura was pregnant by the time the Waughs moved into Piers Court and in March 1938 she gave birth to their first child, Teresa. Two months later, Waugh's last pre-war novel was published. *Scoop!* draws on its author's time as a war correspondent in Abyssinia and fictionalizes the Herbert family as the Boots of Boot Magna.

WORLD WAR II

At the onset of World War II, Waugh was thirty-six. By the end of it, he and Laura would have four children: a fifth, Mary, was born in 1940 but lived for just a day. Continual childbearing took its toll on Laura, who apparently greeted news of her pregnancies with dismay and resignation.[61] Waugh's father was less accepting. When Laura found she was expecting Mary just months after the birth of Auberon, her second child, Arthur remarked tartly: 'The Roman Catholic priests insist upon it.'[62]

Laura's troubles were exacerbated by Waugh's absence at the front. Despite his age he was eager to join up, but faced multiple rejections until he was finally offered a commission in the Royal Marines.

Waugh served in various units and was transferred often during the war, and continued to write and publish novels throughout. The first of these was *Put Out More Flags* (1942), a greyish comedy covering the first few months of war in England. Waugh wrote the novel aboard the *Duchess of Richmond*, on a long crossing home following one of the most harrowing episodes in his wartime service.[63] He had been sent

Waugh in uniform during his World War II service.

with 'Layforce', a commando unit led by Lieutenant-Colonel Robert Laycock, to assist in the evacuation of Crete. How much 'assistance' the unit actually gave, and what exactly happened on that island in 1941, have been the subject of fierce controversy,[64] and the actions of Laycock's troops (himself included) left their mark on Waugh. Little of this anguish, however, found its way into *Put Out More Flags*. Waugh would return to it later.

In June 1943 Arthur Waugh died with, as Evelyn put it, 'disconcerting suddenness'.[65] Alec was in Baghdad serving with the Dorset regiment, and usually lived in America. This left the less-favoured son to take responsibility for their father's estate and care for their mother.[66] Waugh

The Waugh family, *c.* 1947. Evelyn and Laura surrounded (*left to right*) by Teresa, James (on Laura's lap), Auberon (behind), Hatty and Meg (holding cat).

had proved to be a difficult and disruptive officer, and Laycock's superiors seized this opportunity first to reduce his involvement with their unit under the guise of compassionate leave and then, when Waugh wished to return, to sack him on the grounds of slovenliness and insubordination. Not to be deterred, Waugh argued his way into the SAS instead but found little to do there. In winter 1943, he and Christopher Sykes, who was to be his first biographer, arranged for officers at a loose end to undertake parachute training.[67] Waugh broke his leg on the second jump.[68]

It was the second time in Waugh's life that a broken limb prompted him to start a new book. This one had been forming in his mind for a while, and at the beginning of 1944, signed off for three months, he began to write it down. He had a sense that it would be momentous, and soon began referring to the work as his 'Magnum Opus' or 'M.O.'[69] At first he called it *The House of the Faith*, but eventually settled on the title *Brideshead Revisited*. Although most of the action in *Brideshead Revisited* is set elsewhere, its vivid depiction of Oxford – like Waugh's brief residence in the city – took on a significance that far outstripped its duration. It was to be the first of two occasions when Waugh, in the shadow of death, chose to beautify his student memories by transforming them into literature.

Brideshead Revisited was finished in June 1944.[70] With the war now in its last European stages, Waugh was called back to active duty. One of his last missions was to assist Croatian partisans in beating back German forces – during the course of this operation Waugh was involved in a plane crash with Winston Churchill's son Randolph. Both men survived, Randolph with damage to his knees and Waugh with burns to his hands, legs and head. After their recovery they proceeded as planned to Yugoslavia, where at first Waugh was anxious to investigate reports of communist-sponsored mistreatment of Roman Catholics. Soon, however, his concern for Catholic welfare was joined by a slow-burning distress at the plight of Jewish refugees in the country. In this, his compassion took him by surprise.[71]

Waugh finally returned to Laura and his family on 10 September 1945, a 'grey, fly-infested, heavy evening'.[72] He was now father to Teresa, Auberon, Meg and Harriet. *Brideshead Revisited* had been published in May.

BRIDESHEAD AND AFTER

The first edition of *Brideshead Revisited* was 'produced in complete conformity with the authorized economy standards' of wartime publishing.[73] It was an immediate success, and remains Waugh's best-known novel.

Waugh in Hollywood, February 1947, with his favourite actress, Anna May Wong (*left*),
Sir Charles Mendl and Laura.

Stylistically it was a departure from his earlier, satirical works; if descriptions of it as a 'watershed' book are a little overstated,[74] it nonetheless fundamentally altered the public perception of Waugh. It was his first fiction to deal with explicitly Catholic themes. By the end of 1945 he was working on a second, *Helena* (1950). This historical fiction follows St Helena as she searches for the True Cross[75] in a corrupt and decadent, only nominally Christian, Roman Empire. It would take Waugh five years to write.[76]

The lost yet quintessential England evoked in *Brideshead Revisited* sealed the book's popularity in the United States, and Waugh's new-found success there led to several journeys across the Atlantic in the late 1940s. He went to Hollywood to discuss a possible film adaptation of *Brideshead* and made two lecture tours, during which he developed a keen

LEFT Waugh with his
youngest son, Septimus,
in 1955.

interest in both American Catholicism and modern American attitudes
to death.[77] The latter found expression in Waugh's short novel *The Loved
One* (1948), the acerbic style of which recalls his earlier dark comedies.
Waugh also made frequent visits to mainland Europe in these post-war
years, staying with Nancy Mitford in Paris and even attending part of
the Nuremburg Trials.[78] This last experience was one of very few to find
no place in Waugh's published works. Instead, his observations of the
spread of communism across Soviet territories informed the 1947 short
story *Scott-King's Modern Europe*.

Waugh eschewed party politics and went to increasing lengths to
avoid general elections.[79] He was, however, undoubtedly a 'small-c
conservative', believing that the functions of government should be
restricted to defence of the realm, protection of the currency and
safeguarding the inheritance of widows and orphans. Politicians, he said,

gave 'themselves ulcers and [made] themselves ill by doing things that [aren't] their job'. As such he was discomfited for the post-war expansion of the welfare state as 'promising what it can never do'.[80] This unease fed into the dystopian novella *Love Among the Ruins* (1953).

When *Helena* was finally published in 1950 reviews were, to Waugh's bitter disappointment, lukewarm at best.[81] Much better received were his trilogy of wartime novels, *Men at Arms* (1952), *Officers and Gentlemen* (1955) and *Unconditional Surrender* (1961). Here, Waugh's experiences in Crete and Croatia and his near-fatal plane crash are transformed and woven into a framework of epic struggle, disillusionment and self-realization narrated with a late-modernist detachment that borders on the surreal. He later revised the novels and published them as a single volume, *Sword of Honour* (1965). They are still considered the masterpieces of Waugh's mature period.

BELOW Waugh's letters to his daughter Meg (pictured here on their trip to the Caribbean over winter 1961–62) were affectionate and full of fatherly advice.

LATER YEARS

Waugh became increasingly reclusive in his later years, plagued by per-
secution mania and depression. He and Laura had two more sons, James
and Septimus, making three living girls and three boys. Waugh carried
on writing to support the family and, as he complained, to service his
huge tax bills (for which he blamed left-leaning governments). In 1956
the Waughs moved to Combe Florey in Somerset, where Evelyn spent
the school holidays in hiding from his large brood. Yet, while he found
his children's physical presence tiring,[82] Waugh's letters to them are
tolerant, affectionate and replete with fatherly advice.[83] His friendships,
too, were more successful on paper than in person.

Waugh's drinking, which had always been substantial, grew even
heavier. He began with gin in the mornings, moved on to wine in the
evenings, and took large doses of sleeping draught to gain nocturnal
relief from the 'exquisite boredom'[84] of his life. The strategy proved
disastrous when in 1954 the combination of alcohol and paraldehyde

An unusually relaxed Waugh during his 1961–62 Caribbean trip.

The Railway Club reunion, November 1963.
Back row, left to right Desmond Guinness, Robert Boothby, Harold Acton, Henry Harrod, John Sparrow and Auberon Waugh.
Middle row, left to right Sir Roy Harrod, Evelyn Waugh, John Sutro, Cyril Connolly, Giles Fitzherbert, Randal McDonnell, 8th Earl of Antrim, Dominick Harrod, Terence Greenidge and two porters.
Front row, left to right Christopher Sykes, *Brighton Belle* cook and Henry Thynne, 6th Marquess of Bath.

induced bromide poisoning and auditory hallucinations. Waugh's state of mind during this period is partially captured in *The Ordeal of Gilbert Pinfold* (1957), the most autobiographical of his novels, which features a middle-aged author going out of his mind whilst on board a cruise ship.

In the early 1960s Waugh was also distressed by the Catholic Church's modernizing of the Mass service.[85] Waugh took solace from the knowledge that Catholic rites remained unchanging in a chaotic and, it seemed to him, ever more unstable world. Now that consolation was denied him. Despairing of the modern, Waugh instead looked for comfort in his own history. He began *A Little Learning* in 1961, and introduced the memoir with the downbeat, provocative assertion that '[o]nly when one has lost all curiosity about the future has one reached the age to write an autobiography.'[86] His research for the book brought him back into contact with his university cronies and in November 1963 sparked a reunion with Terence Greenidge and many others, but the gathering made Waugh feel even older. The elderly, portly and deaf condition of his friends contrasted cruelly with the image of Oxford he was hard at work to resurrect, and reinforced for him the superiority of the past over the present.[87]

Waugh's autobiography describes his youth as 'the preparation for one trade only; that of an English prose writer'.[88] However, while the material circumstances of his early life did push him towards university and a career in letters, the unique response to Oxford which permeates Waugh's work sprang from more individual factors. His awareness of his brother as the favourite son, his sense of exile at Lancing and his father's perceived mediocrity determined him, on the one hand, to prove himself and, on the other, to kick out against the status quo which had placed him in what he saw as an ignoble position. Oxford provided the perfect environment for both endeavours, encouraging Waugh in personal and artistic experimentation and offering up its idols to be smashed in the process. It was in every sense a formative experience that left its mark throughout his life and literature.

A Little Learning follows its author's life only as far as the mid-1920s. It was intended as the first volume of a longer work,[89] but Waugh died before even its sequel – aptly named *A Little Hope*[90] – was finished. He suffered a massive coronary thrombosis at Combe Florey on Easter Sunday 1966 and was buried in the grounds of his home. His headstone reads simply: 'Evelyn Waugh, Writer'.

OPPOSITE Evelyn Waugh's woodcut of Harold Acton, *Isis*, February 1924.

Evelyn Waugh's City

City of Invention

Waugh claimed to do minimal work at Oxford and, as far as his History degree was concerned, this is accurate. Almost as soon as he ventured beyond the environs of Hertford College he fell in with a crowd of young men somewhat richer than he, and consequently less in need of qualifications. High-born friends like Hugh Lygon and Harold Acton had large personal fortunes to fall back on, and so could afford to indulge their tastes at Oxford however they pleased. For such men, Oxford functioned as a sort of masculine finishing school. It was 'a place to grow up in'[91] or, at most, a place to make the kind of friends that might help one in later life. Their fees helped to fund the scholarships upon which their poorer, cleverer counterparts relied: men like Waugh and his contemporary A.L. Rowse, both supposedly reading History but with radically different attitudes to study.

Waugh's friends were known as the Aesthetes, and Harold Acton was their undisputed leader. He was an Old Etonian, a precociously talented poet and flamboyant dresser. He introduced the famously wide-hemmed 'Oxford Bags' to the University, and appeared to Rowse 'a bird of brilliant plumage'.[92] Next to Acton, Waugh looked positively

OPPOSITE Recently discovered pen-and-ink drawing by Evelyn Waugh, 1929. Harold Acton's novel *Humdrum!* can be seen in the picture.

The voters were all tipsy. I performed no secretarial duties. My appointment was a characteristic fantasy of the place, and after a time I had a tiff and either resigned or was deposed – I forget which. My predecessor in the office, Loveday, had left the university suddenly to study black magic. He died in mysterious circumstances at Cefalu in Alistair Crowley's community and his widow, calling herself 'Tiger Woman' figured for some time in the popular Press, where she made 'disclosures' of the goings-on at Cefalu.

The building which housed the Hypocrites was timbered and, I think, genuinely Tudor; it has now been demolished and its site is unidentifiable. One ascended narrow stairs (rather as in London one descends to Pratt's) into a rich smell of onions and grilling meat. Usually the constable on the beat was standing in the kitchen, helmet in one hand, a mug of beer in the other. Above and beyond the kitchen were two large rooms. I saw the transition by which dart targets and shove-halfpenny boards gave place to murals by Mr Oliver Messel (a frequent visitor from London) and Robert Byron. There was a piano. Folk music and glees gave place to jazz and, more in the fashion, to Victorian drawing-room ballads.

180

horrid place

Silly lot of hippie youths.

parochial; his new friend, whose family home was in Italy, 'brought with him the air of the connoisseurs of Florence and the innovators of Paris, of Berenson and of Gertrude Stein, Magnasco and T.S. Eliot'. As a young man he was not, Waugh said, 'learned', but 'vividly alive to every literary and artistic fashion'.[93] It was Acton whose reading of Osbert and Edith Sitwell's poetry through a megaphone[94] inspired *Brideshead Revisited*'s parallel scene of Anthony Blanche reciting *The Waste Land* 'in languishing, sobbing tones'.[95]

The Aesthetes represented a way of life far removed from that of Rowse. An extremely gifted, working-class historian (his father was barely literate), Rowse had almost forfeited the only county scholarship for the whole of Cornwall on account of his left-wing politics. To him, Waugh and his friends were simply 'wastrels' who drank away

OPPOSITE Historian A.L. Rowse's verdict on Waugh, as annotated in his personal copy of *A Little Learning*, 1964.

RIGHT Waugh as the dean of Balliol in Terence Greenidge's *The Scarlet Woman*, 1924.

the opportunities life handed them. Rowse annotated a personal copy of *A Little Learning* with his observations on Waugh: 'silly', 'spoiled' and 'le[d] away by snobbery'.[96]

Although conventionally work-shy, Acton and Waugh were still productive at university. They may have been often hung-over, but they were rarely idle. Acton, for example, founded the *Oxford Broom*, modelled on the Continental *Broom: An International Magazine of the Arts*, while Waugh, as well as writing and acting in Terence Greenidge's *The Scarlet Woman* (1924), contributed more than thirty-seven articles and regular columns, thirty-two pieces of graphic art and six short stories to the *Isis*, *Cherwell* and the *Oxford Fortnightly Review* as well providing editorial support and a front cover for the *Oxford Broom*.[97] Many of these pieces are signed with Waugh's pseudonym, 'Scaramel'. Waugh also created personalized bookplates for his friends and lovers[98] and, by the time he left university, was producing occasional jacket designs for his father at Chapman & Hall.[99]

These are conservative numbers. The content of student magazines was generated by a handful of contributors, and much of it is unsigned. This mock-advert for Keble, for example, works on a mixture of sarcasm and incongruity that would not be out of place in Waugh's early comedies and shares their fascination with new, truncated styles of communication. Keble was a relatively new college, founded in 1870, and stood a little outside the main concentration of colleges between High Street and Broad Street. It was thus evidently funny to pretend it was in the country:

LEFT Waugh's bookplate design for Alastair Graham, *c.* 1923.

RIGHT Cover design for the OUDS production of *The Rhesus*, June 1923. .

DON'T RISK YOUR HEALTH
By staying in the enervating Oxford climate.
go to
— KEBLE —
within easy taxi-drive of Oxford.
salubrious climate.
delightful surroundings.[100]

In a closed world like Oxford it is inevitable that close-knit groups of writer-friends might develop similar styles and share a sense of humour, so attribution must always be tentative; nevertheless, there are hints of a Wavian mindset in dozens of throwaway pieces of magazine copy like this. It is especially likely that the issues of the *Isis* produced in the spring (or Hilary) term of 1924 carry unsigned work by Waugh, as he was serving as Arthur Tandy's subeditor at the time.[101]

Much of Waugh's student output has been dismissed as either immature or only interesting to a limited audience of fellow students. However, at Oxford Waugh was hard at work honing his skills in social observation, and this unique body of literary and visual material is not merely an echo chamber for contemporary modes and mores. Rather, it reflected that little society back to itself with the amused and incisive clarity of a commentator who stood with one foot outside it, and one foot within.

When Waugh went up to university he saw himself primarily as a visual artist, not a writer. The conviction grew during his student years, and when he left in the summer of 1924 it was to enrol in art school rather than to pursue a literary career. This venture failed, as did his attempts to learn carpentry and the art of printmaking, but Waugh's interest in illustrating his personal and published writings continued. His first three novels were published with his own illustrations: *Decline and Fall* and *Black Mischief* incorporate Waugh's line drawings (and in the case of *Decline and Fall* the front cover too) while *Vile Bodies* boasts a boldly graphic frontispiece which encapsulates the frenetic aesthetic mood of both the book and its times. The later novella *Love Among the Ruins* is also 'decorated' by the author, and in 1963 Waugh suggested providing his own sketches for *A Little Learning*.[102]

Image had accompanied text in Waugh's work since his first excursions into diary-keeping at the age of seven, when he drew his maths teacher Mr Cooper with an obscenely large head and oversized cane.[103] This was normal enough for a small child, but Waugh kept up the practice in his diaries – which run to one entry a day for much of his time at Lancing – right up to sixth form and his departure for Oxford. The unfortunate Mr Cooper was followed the next year by Waugh's depiction of his own appendectomy, in which a triumphant surgeon holds a pair of forceps and a disquietingly long knife above a prone, white-faced boy.[104] From these childhood sketches Waugh progressed to pen-and ink vignettes of schoolboy fights, football games and training exercises with the Lancing army corps.[105]

As Waugh's style developed he began to emulate specific illustrators and designers whose work he admired. For example, in March 1921 forty schoolboys were confirmed in Lancing College Chapel. Waugh,

OPPOSITE As well as
illustrating several of
his published works,
Waugh also rearranged
nineteenth-century
drawings to produce
subversive montages
for *Love Among the Ruins*
(Chapman & Hall, 1953).

RIGHT Waugh's impression
of his appendectomy
in his childhood diary,
10 June 1912.

BELOW 'Mr Cooper's
Classroom' from
Waugh's childhood diary,
c. 10 September 1911.

Bishop imagined 'as a dressed-up coloured thing like a Dulac figure' from Waugh's Lancing College diary, 15 March 1921.

then on the point of declaring himself an atheist, was disturbed by the ceremony and described the bishop as 'a dressed-up coloured thing like a Dulac figure and gloomy threatening masters and provosts all round'. He produced a heavily cross-hatched, squat and angular caricature of the bishop to match.[106]

'Dulac' was Edmund Dulac, a popular French artist whose Gothic illustrations appeared in Edgar Allan Poe's *The Bells and Other Poems*[107] as well as his own *Fairy Book* (1916).[108] His style reflected the decadent yet clean-lined aesthetic of art nouveau, which also informed the more graphic work of Aubrey Beardsley. Waugh wrote on Beardsley during his Oxford scholarship exam, and had long been familiar with the artist for the unlikely reason that both his and Arthur Waugh's work appear in John Lane's first *Yellow Book* of 1894. Waugh senior's contribution was a blameless essay in literary criticism.[109] Beardsley's front cover, on the other hand, displays a sexual ambivalence typical of the artist. It features a masked man and woman apparently enjoying a carnival but whose smiles convey both the playfulness and threatening undercurrent associated with carnival space.[110]

Dulac's Gothicism and Beardsley's playful menace are both discernible in the artwork Waugh produced at Oxford, as is the influence of the sculptor and woodcut designer Eric Gill. Waugh had been taken as a child to visit a self-sufficient artists' colony founded by Gill, and later went to boarding school near the site.[111] Like Beardsley's, Gill's work is sexually subversive but Waugh's woodcuts, for which he became well known, resemble Gill's in appearance more than tone. His series of 'Seven Deadly Sins' for *Cherwell*, for example, combine Gill's proto-futuristic line and shape with Beardsley's sinister overtones; they are not explicit, yet they are unsettling. In 'The Wanton Way of those that Corrupt the

BELOW LEFT Aubrey Beardsley's cover design for the first issue of *The Yellow Book*, April 1894.

BELOW RIGHT Waugh, 'The Seven Deadly Sins. No III. The Wanton Way of those that Corrupt the Very Young', *Cherwell*, 1923.

ABOVE Waugh, 'Bertram, Ludovic and Ann', *Isis*, 1923.

RIGHT Stuart Boyle's frontispiece illustration of Waugh's *The Loved One* (Chapman & Hall, 1948).

Very Young', for example, a top-hatted, striped-trousered man crouches down to a little girl in pigtails with an air that implies a much darker kind of corruption than that suggested in an accompanying poem (*not* by Waugh) relating the death of Socrates.[112]

One of the funniest pieces of Waugh's visual satire featured three characters named Bertram, Ludovic and Ann, who appeared as an illustration to the *Isis*'s 'Children's Corner'.[113] They accompany a spoof open letter from 'Auntie Ermyntrude', also written by Waugh. Both text and image parody the didacticism of Edwardian children's literature, employing a conversational narrative style which addresses young readers directly (Ermyntrude speaks to her readers as 'my dears') and co-opting anthropomorphized animals to make moral points. However, while in classic tales these animals might be deliberately exotic, like J.M. Barrie's crocodile in *Peter Pan*, or else familiar woodland creatures, like *Peter Rabbit*,[114] Bertram, Ludovic and Ann are, respectively, a bumblebee, a snail and an ant. In Waugh's illustration, a young man is sitting up in bed; Ludovic and Ann are crawling across his covers while Bertram hovers above them, level with his face. Instead of being delighted with their company, the man looks unnerved. From the text, we learn that 'the Pets'

have disturbed the editor of the *Isis* 'in bed, at half-past twelve', and that Bertram 'wanted to sting the naughty editor outright' for his slovenliness. Waugh's cartoon is both silly and disturbing. The insects have absurdly dignified names, and by magnifying Ludovic to the size of the *Isis* editor's torso Waugh renders him and his friends not warm and whimsical but grotesque and terrifying. A sting from Bertram could kill the unhappy editor. Years later, Waugh would choose the artist Stuart Boyle to illustrate his satiric novella *The Loved One*; Boyle's caricatures and illuminated letters recall the combination of Gothic excess, threat and humour Waugh learnt from Dulac and Beardsley and tailored to his own aesthetic during his Oxford days.

The *Isis* ran a regular feature called 'Isis Idol', which singled out a leading member of the University for praise. In February 1924

Waugh contributed a piece on Harold Acton, which acted as a mini-manifesto for the *Oxford Broom*. The magazine was 'badly needed', Waugh said, and acted as 'a magnificent tonic for the sullen mind of the literary undergraduate'. The *Broom* was so named because it intended to sweep away the stale cultural ideas that had, before Acton's arrival, created a 'foetid atmosphere' at Oxford and usher in the new.[115] Under Acton's tutelage, Waugh's visual frame of reference grew to include aspects of continental Europe's new Modernist movements. The cover he designed for the *Oxford Broom* in April 1923 still has much in common with Gill's aesthetic, but its intricately piled mythical beasts, waves, brooms and tumbling figures also owe a debt to both Vorticism and Dada. A later cartoon headed 'Cornish Landscape with White Cow in Thought. E.W. 1924'[116] mocks the pastoral tradition evoked in its title with ruined castles, and distant factory chimneys planted in the centre of the top third of the canvas. The cow, an animal not usually known for its thoughtfulness, is looking away from us and only the back of her head is visible. Both designs are iconoclastic and disjointed, both weirdly threatening.

LEFT Waugh, cover design for the *Oxford Broom*, first appearing April 1923.

ABOVE Waugh, 'Cornish Landscape with White Cow in Thought. E.W. 1924', *Cherwell*, February 1924.

Critical reception of Waugh's graphic art has been coloured by the dismissive attitude of its originator. In *A Little Learning*, Waugh claims that at Oxford his pen was in demand largely because no one else bothered to draw at all.[117] And yet Waugh's most ambitious designs found their way into the *London Mercury*[118] and were printed in Clifford Bax's *Golden Hind*.[119] As well as the one-off pieces Waugh produced, at least ten of his designs were used by the magazines as regular column headers, and in the case of *Broom* and *Cherwell* the front cover too. Much of Waugh's artwork was also used for years after he went down.

Waugh's column header for the Union, first appearing in *Isis*, January 1923.

Waugh's first regular written copy was a column reporting Union debates in the *Oxford Fortnightly Review*, a magazine for which he also acted as business manager.[120] As a schoolboy visitor to the University he'd thought the speakers no better than his Lancing *Dilettanti*,[121] but in practice he found it difficult to form elegant, sustained arguments in the debating hall and his speeches made little impact.[122] The column, however, prospered.

Most of Waugh's substantial Oxford journalism appeared in the *Isis* during his term as subeditor. This period covered Waugh's two contributions to the 'Isis Idol' series (although the authorship of the Cruttwell piece is disputed), a musing leader on the Oxford University Dramatic Society's production of *Hamlet* and – most importantly of all– a regular film column entitled 'Seen in the Dark'.

Donat Gallagher, the editor of numerous volumes of Waugh's essays, articles and reviews, questions the attribution of 'Isis Idol No. 596: C.R.M.F. Cruttwell, M.A.' because of its departure from the author's usual style. Gallagher does, however, suggest that as the magazine's subeditor Waugh could have collaborated in the preparation of its content, with which he would have been in perfect sympathy.[123] The bigger mystery is how, either for editing or originating an article which ironically praises a college don for drinking and swearing while excusing his ugliness, Waugh managed to avoid being sent down. His friend Gerald Gardiner, who assumed the *Isis* subeditorship the term after Waugh, suffered precisely that fate for passing an article which vehemently criticized the social restrictions placed on female undergraduates.[124]

Popular cinema was a new form of mass entertainment in the 1920s, and the *Isis*'s weekly review column was an innovation. Waugh's summaries, narrated with a characteristic weary flippancy, are rich in historical detail which brings the early cinema to life. During *The Enemies of Women*, for example, we learn that the silent explosion of a bomb on-screen was enhanced in the auditorium with a real-life bang and copious smoke. This early example of immersive theatre was so effective (and so unexpected) that it caused a small panic.[125]

Waugh reviewed Oxford's film offerings primarily in visual terms and, although he would remain interested in cinema throughout his life, for him silent film held the most exciting aesthetic potential. This was a view shared by Virginia Woolf, and the two writers' thoughts on film have much in common. Both, for example, had a distaste for literalist cinematography and hated the popular flamboyant, overly demonstrative acting style then in vogue; in one of his reviews, Waugh also complained about the 'pretentious generalizations and mixed metaphors' of film subtitles. The 'real charm of the Cinema', he wrote, 'is in the momentary pictures and situations which appear'. Waugh compared these fleeting visual effects, such as a 'violent struggle in [a] strange, unmoving jungle of monstrous animals', to the fragmented and macabre imagery of Edith Sitwell's early poetry.[126] A few years later in 1926, Woolf would locate cinema's emotive and representational power even more conceptually, in an imperfection of the film reel that projected a 'black line wriggling' in the corner of the screen. For Waugh and Woolf, silent film promised 'innumerable symbols for emotions'[127] that remained unrealized when this 'new and vital Art' was eclipsed by the talkie.[128]

Waugh's slim output of short stories whilst at Oxford pales in comparison with his journalism and graphic art of the same period. Of the six stories, all of which were published in 1923, the first four concern either real or imagined murders and five feature undergraduate characters and settings. In 'Portrait of Young Man with Career',[129] Waugh and his boyfriend Richard Pares appear under their real names. 'Portrait' was the earliest story and, along with its successors 'Anthony, Who Sought Things That Were Lost'[130] and 'Edward of Unique Achievement',[131] is an exercise in wish-fulfilment. The first narrative is a comedy of manners, in which Evelyn is rudely kept from his bath by Jeremy, a thinly veiled caricature of Waugh's Lancing acquaintance Hugh Molson.[132] Jeremy, patently out for his own interests, fails to recognize Evelyn's social cues as he smokes his reluctant host's cigarettes and badgers him to introduce him to Pares ('I feel he is a man to know'). While forced to listen to Jeremy's boring talk, Evelyn fantasizes about braining him with a poker.

In the following two stories murder really is committed: in 'Edward' the hero stabs a Cruttwell figure named Mr Curtis, while in 'Anthony' an adulterous wife is murdered by her jealous husband. 'Edward' is mischievous, and displays the same cutting social observation as 'Portrait' (Mr Curtis, we are told, 'had that habit, more fitting for a house master than a don, of continuing to read or write some few words after his visitors entered, in order to emphasize his superiority'). 'Anthony' on the other hand was, according to an older Waugh, inspired by a 'preposterously spurious' novel by James Branch Cabell: *Jurgen, A Comedy of Justice*.[133] Presumably Waugh's later objection to the book was founded in its blasphemous irreverence to the pope and flirtation with black magic. Its main influence on 'Anthony' seems to be through its irreverent parody of courtly love and Arthurian legend, which translate in Waugh's story into a Malloryesque setting and a 'mannered' style that Selina Hastings associates with 'Wildean pastiche' and Martin Stannard with the King James Bible and 'Websterian cruelty'.[134] Both biographers note that its composition coincides with the break-up of Waugh and Pares's relationship. As such, Anthony's strangling of the false Lady Elizabeth could be a revenge fantasy. This interpretation would cast the dean of Balliol as Anthony's ugly and depraved love rival, and hint at a sexual rather than intellectual motive for Urquhart's rescuing of Pares 'for a life of scholarship'.[135] There is no evidence that this was the case, despite Waugh's insinuations to that effect.[136]

The relative paucity of these early stories notwithstanding, the narratives do foreground some preoccupations of Waugh's mature works. Hastings has identified their shared 'fascination for murder, madness and the grotesque';[137] to this might be added their contempt for those who set too much store by their dignity and their author's delight in exacting literary revenge on his enemies. In 'Anthony', moreover, Waugh's fear of social disorder and the barbarity of the masses have their first outing. The best of these stories look forward to Waugh's humorously, yet cruelly accurate, reflections of human failing.

In February 1924 OUDS staged *Hamlet*. Waugh wrote an editorial in the *Isis* to mark the occasion, in which he suggests that *Hamlet* was no madder than any other undergraduate and that the play was, at heart, an exploration of the Oxford condition. 'From any window in Oxford it would not be hard to pick out twenty Osrics and two hundred Horatios,' he wrote, 'and surely Polonius himself, napkin in hand, may be seen hobbling from dinner to the Senior Common Room?' It did not surprise

Waugh's frontispiece for *Cherwell*, first appearing August 1923.

Waugh that Shakespeare did not, so far as we know, spend any time at Oxford. He observed in his editorial that 'foreigner[s]' typically wrote better accounts of university life than their 'native' counterparts. He knew that it was hard to occupy the stage and the pit at the same time.[138]

Waugh took an active social role at Oxford, and was then more in the thick of things than at any other time in his life. And yet he still understood the importance of critical distance. This is nowhere clearer than in his design for the front page of *Cherwell*, created after his friend John Sutro took over ownership in August 1923. Waugh's frontispiece features five Oxford 'types' drawn as marionettes: a limp-wristed and wide-trousered aesthete, a beer-swilling 'hearty', a don and a Union speaker are joined on the far left by an insensible figure, his back to the audience, slouching forward and on his puppet strings.[139] The illustration was hugely popular and was used, with some revision in 1929, until 1940.[140]

Waugh's marionettes are performing for the viewer's entertainment, just as *Cherwell* lampooned Oxford characters for the enjoyment of its readers. Waugh's sinister undercurrent is still there. One puppet is limp, and all are lifeless; the don hangs by his neck, as if executed. In its way, the drawing is just as violent as Waugh's first stories and warns that satire is a destructive as well as a comedic force. It may deny its victims their interiority, and reduce them to performing apes.[141] Waugh marked his first victims at Oxford, and the list would grow throughout his career. But if satire does flatten or even destroy its subjects, then Waugh's image also asks whose fault, ultimately, that is. By depicting Oxford's 'types' as puppets Waugh also critiques their lack of personal agency, and implies that the outside viewer possesses an autonomy which they do not. If they will not think for themselves then they must take the consequences.

Much of Waugh's student art and writing is, by definition, ephemeral, and its lightness of touch is fitting for the publications in which it appeared. When Waugh began to be published outside Oxford, he would be criticized for the oddly insubstantial quality of his works, but his surface frothiness topped a deep and troubling engagement with human nature. The fact that Waugh's weakest area of student writing would become his greatest strength suggests that, at Oxford, his important work might have been going on below the surface: observations originally made in one medium might find final expression in quite another.

City of Memory

The novelist does not come to his desk devoid of experience and memory. His raw material is compounded of all he has seen and done.[142]

When Waugh's autobiography, *A Little Learning*, was published in 1964, reviewers were less inclined to connect it with its immediate predecessors as with a novel he'd written twenty years before. The Catholic arts periodical *The Cresset*, for example, noted 'some signs ... of the future author of *Brideshead Revisited*' in Waugh's narrative but 'far fewer of the rollicking creator of *Black Mischief*, *Vile Bodies*, or *Put Out More Flags*'.[143] Given that both *Brideshead Revisited* and *A Little Learning* deal with Oxford in the early 1920s, the comparison suggests itself easily enough, and between them these two texts are responsible for the image of Oxford most immediately recognized as 'Wavian'. This Oxford, as Charles Ryder famously describes in *Brideshead Revisited*, is 'a city of aquatint':

> her autumnal mists, her grey springtime, and the rare glory of her summer days – such as that day – when the chestnut was in flower and the bells rang out high and clear over her gables and cupolas, exhaled the soft vapours of a thousand years of learning.[144]

OPPOSITE Manuscript of *Brideshead Revisited*, 1944, with the name 'Alastair' originally in place of Sebastian.

you sure this is the best way of dealing with it?" // "It's my mother's way." "Well you have a cocktail now that stairs." // "It would choke me". // ~~start~~ I had my old room next to Sebastian's. He was out of the bath as on my way back to dress I stopped at his door and, as I always did, entered without knocking. He was sitting by the open window and he started guiltily when he heard me and put down a tooth glass. // "Oh it's you. You gave me a... So you got a drink," I said // "I don't know what you mean" // "For Christ's sake", I said, "You don't have me. You might offer me some" // "It's just something I had in my flask. I've finished it now." // "What's you going. A lot. I'll tell you sometime". // I dressed and called in for Sebastian but he was still sitting as I left him by his fire. // Julia was alone in the drawing-room. // "Well," I asked, "what's going on." // "Oh just another potion. Sebastian got tight again so we've all got keep an eye on him. It is too tedious." // "It's pretty too" // "Well, it's his fault. Why can't he behave like anyone else? Talking of keeping an eye on people — Samgrass? Charles, do you notice anything at all fishy about him?" // "Very fishy. Do you think your...?" // "Mummy only sees what suits her. She can't have the household under surveillance. I'm causing you know". // "I didn't know", I said, adding humbly ~~apologetically~~, "I've only just come from Paris" for it was at time, to make a girl ~~to support think~~ that any trouble she might be in was not widely notorious. // It was an evening ~~among Julia's friends~~ gloom. We dined in the painted parlour. Sebastian was late, and so painfully ... that I think it was in all our minds that he would make some sort of low-comedy entrance; when he came, of course, it was with perfect propriety; he apologised, sat in the empty place and allowed to resume his monologue uninterrupted and, it seemed, unheard. Druses, patriarchs, ikons, the bugs, Armenians, curious dishes of goat and sheeps' eyes, French and Turkish officials — all the catalogue of near was provided for our amusement. // I watched the champagne go round the table. When it came to Sebastian he

Wilcox

have whiskey please" and I saw ~~Wilkins~~ glance on his head to Lady Marchmain and saw give a tiny, hardly nod. // They used ~~to~~ small individual spirit decanters [at Brideshead] ~~that~~ and we always place, full, before anyone who as was [which held about quarter of a bottle] now put before Sebastian and in an instant all our eyes were barely a third full. Sebastian raised it up deliberately, tilted it, looked at it, and then in silence poured the

an expert ~~Sebastian~~ Sebastian's

his glass when it covered two fingers. We all began talking at once fro that for a moment Mr Samgrass found ~~himself~~ talking to no one, telling the candlesticks about the Maronites, but soon we fell silent again while Lady Marchmain and Julia left the room. // "Don't be long, Bridey" she said at the door, as she always ...ing we had no inclination to delay. Our glasses were filled with the port and the decanter at once tak

That this image should have such enduring power is curious for two reasons. First, in both texts the majority of the action occurs away from Oxford. Charles Ryder, for instance, is quickly whisked off from university, first to Brideshead Castle and then to Venice. He also spends time in London and the United States, and a significant portion of the narrative takes place during an Atlantic crossing. Likewise, as Peter Quennell remarked in a catty memoir of Evelyn at Oxford, his former friend's university days make up just a fifth of *A Little Learning*.[145] In literature as in life, Waugh's Oxford experiences appear to have taken on a significance that transcends their brief temporal – or textual – duration.

The second curiosity lies in the fact that Waugh also wrote about Oxford immediately following his departure from the city. Both his first story to be published outside the student magazines and his first novel depict Oxford in great, unflattering, detail. It might be imagined that the later Wavian vision of Oxford has thrived in afterlife because the years that separate Waugh's personal experience of his subject matter from its literary representation afford a critical distance which allows for a more rounded, realistic portrayal. There are grains of truth in this. Waugh's earlier writings are, perhaps, fuelled by the bitterness of finding himself ejected, before time, from Oxford's 'rare glory'. However, while *Brideshead Revisited* and *A Little Learning* are more realist than the earlier fictions, they are not realistic. Their appeal does not lie in a documentary account of what life was really like in 1920s' Oxford, but what Waugh first expected and, later, remembered it to be.

The nostalgic, idealized representations of Oxford in *Brideshead Revisited* and (to a lesser extent) *A Little Learning* make a good starting point for a discussion of the centrality of memory to Waugh's works, spirituality and sense of personal identity. The ways in which Waugh's and his friends' reminiscences are utilized, honoured and protected in

these books elucidate a world-view in which meaning is located in continuity of personal experience and unbroken connections with the past.
There is a conservatism inherent in this perspective, which in Waugh's
case has often been elided with a simple case of snobbery: a middle-class
boy comes to Oxford, makes some posh friends and adopts their ways
of life as his own.[146] Delving deeper into Waugh's Oxford complicates
this view, adding some much-needed light and shade to an assessment
whose bluntness should not be mistaken for accuracy.

Brideshead Revisited was published in 1945. It would soon become
Waugh's most famous novel, and remains so today. It is narrated from
the vantage point of England in World War II by Charles Ryder, an army
officer, who finds himself billeted at Brideshead Castle, home to the
Catholic Flyte family. Ryder is transported back to his undergraduate days
in Oxford, where he first meets the endearingly naive Sebastian Flyte.
The two boys embark on a 'romantic friendship'[147] and Charles is initially
embraced by the Flyte family, only to be banished by Sebastian's mother,
Lady Marchmain, for encouraging her son's alcoholism. Years later,
Sebastian has run away to Morocco and Charles re-encounters Sebastian's
sister Julia. Charles and Julia, both now married to other people, begin an
affair. They divorce their spouses and agree to marry, but Julia is called
back to the Church by her father's deathbed re-acceptance of Catholicism
and renounces her love for Charles. The story ends back with Charles the
soldier at Brideshead Castle where, in the family chapel, the tabernacle
flame has been relit and burns 'anew among the old stones'.[148]

Brideshead was published in a period of great austerity in Britain.
Rationing was biting hard, bomb sites punctuated city landscapes, and
Waugh was not the only one to believe that the institution of country
houses like Brideshead Castle was gone forever. In such an environment,
he reflected in a later preface to the novel, he gave way to a luxuriousness

of language and description that contrasted with the grim realities of contemporary life; with 'the period of soya beans and Basic English'.[149] Waugh's yearning for a more optimistic and innocent past caught the mood of the nation, much as his satirical comedies of fashionable society had done fifteen years before. He wrote *Brideshead* as a hymn to a world which he thought was disappearing, both socially and materially. His task as a writer was analogous to that of Charles Ryder, who tours England making 'portraits of houses that were soon to be deserted or debased'.[150]

Waugh wanted his novel to exhibit 'the operation of divine grace on a group of diverse but closely connected characters'[151] and its structure can be read as Charles's progression from a boyish, idealized love for Sebastian to a mature, more considered affection for Julia to, finally and tentatively, a spiritual love for the Catholic Church.[152] This trajectory is implied rather than explicit in the narrative and, in popular experience of the novel, Waugh's intended meditation on grace and faith is often eclipsed by Charles's euphoric description of his and Sebastian's student years.

Charles goes up to Oxford, as Waugh did, in 1922. He takes ground-floor rooms in the front quad of his college. Waugh's second set of rooms were in the same position in Hertford College, and there is some evidence that the event which sparks Charles and Sebastian's friendship had a less glamorous basis in fact. According to Selina Hastings, one night a drunken young man 'walked shakily over to Evelyn's open window, leaned inside, and without saying a word was sick on his carpet'.[153] In *Brideshead*, Sebastian wanders over to Charles's window, looks at him for 'a moment with unseeing eyes and then, leaning forward well into the room', is sick.[154] The next day, consumed with remorse, he orders enough flowers to fill Charles's rooms and invites him to lunch.

Waugh lends many of his biographical circumstances to Ryder, but he is not a self-portrait. As Waugh's beautifying of the vomit incident suggests, the narrative tends to expunge or transform his seedier Oxford experiences. Ryder is neither burdened with Waugh's mishaps nor tarred with the worst excesses of his undergraduate behaviour. He gets drunk, but never smashes up the pub in which he drinks; he does not shout obscenities under dons' windows, and when he is involved in drink-driving Sebastian is at the wheel; Charles sits in the back.

This last example shows how Waugh's construction of Charles's world not only heightens its romance but also allows for his protagonist to function as a narrative conduit. Although some observers complained that the resulting character is too boring,[155] Charles's nondescript nature is also crucial to the novel's broad appeal. He is both a cypher and an everyman with whom a wide spectrum of readers can identify, whether they have attended Oxford or not. The romance of his early manhood resides not, per se, in the University but rather in Charles's rhapsodic evocation of the life it fostered and what the setting is made to represent. In *Mad World: Evelyn Waugh and the Secrets of Brideshead*, Paula Byrne is careful to point out that while in the first edition of *Brideshead* Charles hymns 'the soft vapours of a thousand years of learning', Waugh later revised this to the more appropriate 'soft airs of centuries of youth'.[156] This, ultimately, is what animates *Brideshead* and explains why the novel's progression from naive to experienced to divine love has proved problematic for some readers: Waugh is so eloquent on the beauty of lost youth, hope and *joie de vivre* that the novel's closing promise of spiritual comfort can be less convincing than its glowing evocation of the past.

This disparity, it might be argued, is the whole point. The consolations of faith are not obvious as the joys, or even the memory, of youth is obvious. They are, however, profound and lasting, where earthly happiness is superficial and fleeting. Waugh gestures towards this distinction in a letter to the literary critic Desmond MacCarthy, where he describes Anthony Blanche, the epitome of bright young Oxford, as 'obscene and sterile'.[157]

In 1981 Granada Television aired an ambitious, eleven-part serial of *Brideshead Revisited*. Its script dramatized the novel practically verbatim, and Castle Howard did service as Brideshead Castle. Charles Ryder was played by Jeremy Irons, and Sir Laurence Olivier appeared as Lord Marchmain. The social context was curiously similar to that of the book; England had recently suffered the 1978–79 Winter of Discontent, where widespread industrial strikes coincided with the coldest winter for fifteen years, and a severe global recession contributed to mass unemployment. As in 1945, the conditions were ripe for escapism and the series was a runaway success. Derek Granger, the producer of the series, remembered that 'shop windows were filled with Brideshead fashion' and viewers hosted 'Brideshead fancy dress parties'.[158] This was double nostalgia: a wartime hunger for the exuberance of the 1920s was resurrected as an antidote, albeit for only an hour a week, to the harsh economic climate of the early 1980s.

Such was the romantic pull of *Brideshead*'s 'city of aquatint' that it did not just overshadow Waugh's religious themes but also the 'real' Oxford of Waugh's later autobiography, *A Little Learning*.[159] In a body of work notable for plots and characters drawn from life, the book has distinction as his only full-length, non-fictional memoir. Waugh intended it as the first of three volumes, but died eighteen months after its publication.

Waugh's original plan was for this volume to cover the first three decades of his life,[160] but he found composition difficult and stopped the narrative in his early twenties. The first chapter, 'Heredity', discusses Waugh's great-great-grandfathers and their descendants, before the narrative moves through his childhood in Hampstead and schooling at Lancing College. 'Never a Palinode' chronicles Waugh's two and a half

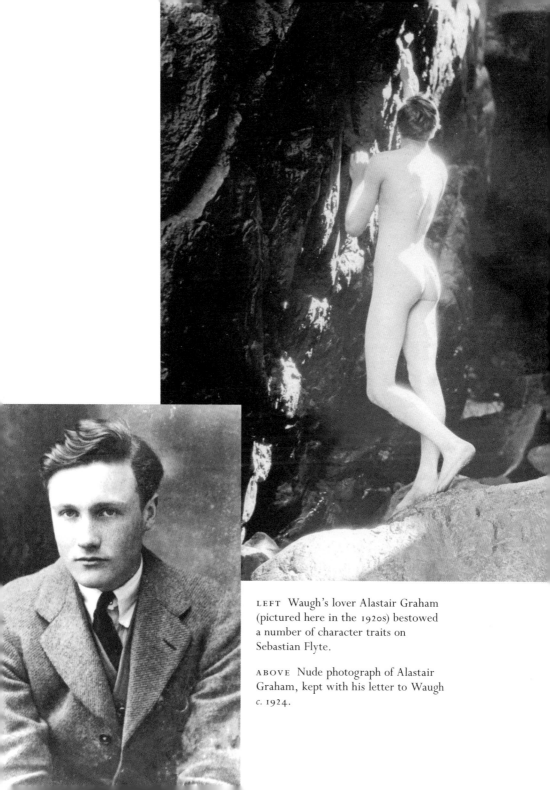

LEFT Waugh's lover Alastair Graham (pictured here in the 1920s) bestowed a number of character traits on Sebastian Flyte.

ABOVE Nude photograph of Alastair Graham, kept with his letter to Waugh *c.* 1924.

years at Oxford. The final chapter narrates Waugh's unhappy experiences post-university at art school and, latterly, as a master at a remote public school in Wales, before concluding with a failed suicide attempt in 1925.

Waugh used 'Never a Palinode' to set the record straight about the supposed originals for his fictional creations, but some readers interpreted his 'long cast of characters'[161] as little more than 'self-indulgence'[162] or 'name-dropping'.[163] His clarification of Harold Acton's tangential relationship to Anthony Blanche, moreover, is arguably duller than either the real-life Acton or the fictional Blanche[164] and led 'many a Waugh admirer' to wish 'that Evelyn would forget about biographies and concentrate on writing another *Brideshead*'.[165] These perceptions of dullness were exacerbated by the book's reticence in more sensitive areas; Waugh remained tight-lipped, for example, about the much stronger connection between Alastair Graham and Sebastian Flyte.[166] Graham was by now a total recluse, estranged from both Waugh and the world,[167] and appeared in *A Little Learning* only under the pseudonym Hamish Lennox.

Consideration for the feelings of others and for the law precluded *A Little Learning* from indulging in truly candid portraiture,[168] and the book is most telling in what remains concealed. Waugh wrote to all the Oxford friends with whom he was still in touch asking permission to use their names in the autobiography. Only two refused: Lord Molson, then Hugh Molson, and Lord Ponsonby of Shulbrede, then Matthew Ponsonby.[169] Waugh thought Molson's attitude typical of his general pompousness and repaid him with the thinnest of veilings, which according to one reviewer 'barely conceal[ed] the identity of a prominent member of the Conservative party' (presumably afraid of libel, he did not name Molson either).[170]

During the writing of *A Little Learning* Waugh found that his memory was fading, and so when he was seeking permission from his friends he also asked them to help fill in the blanks of his Oxford life. None of them was infallible either, and so Waugh's requests for information could result in odd exchanges. Most curious of all was an affair involving John Sutro, *Cherwell*, the Oxford Union and, as in a defining moment of *Brideshead Revisited*, some vomit. Waugh remembered that when Sutro made his debut as a speaker at the Union, he chose to calm his nerves with Dutch courage. He got so drunk that he was unable to speak coherently, sat down on the committee bench and, as Waugh's first draft reads, 'as though in comment on the succeeding speaker, was quietly & neatly sick between his knees'.[171] Waugh wrote to Sutro summarizing the passage, and asking if he could use his name in connection with the episode. Sutro replied giving both his permission and a rival account of the 'inglorious incident', in which he applauded himself after speaking, then staggered out of the Union and became 'unwell' in Oriel Street.[172] Waugh promised to put the record straight, and also incorporated Sutro's self-applause into the finished book. 'My memory plays me tricks', he wrote. 'I was sure you were sick in the debating hall.'[173]

Waugh had a name for this kind of delusion: a 'Pinfold state'.[174] This was a joking reference to his semi-autobiographical novel *The Ordeal of Gilbert Pinfold* (1957), in which the protagonist begins to see and hear things that are not there. The 'ordeal' begins innocently, if embarrassingly enough, when a friend sends Pinfold a beautiful Victorian washstand. Pinfold is convinced that the present has been delivered incomplete, and insists that a missing tap must either be found or adequately compensated for. He appeals to his friend for corroboration, only to learn that 'there never had been any tap such as Mr Pinfold described'.[175] The incident was drawn almost exactly from life. John Betjeman had sent Waugh just such a washstand for his fiftieth birthday; Waugh was able to send Betjeman a 'detailed drawing' of a 'small serpentine bronze pipe', which, it transpired, did not exist.[176]

The displacing of some vomit, forty years after the event, from Oriel Street to the Oxford Union was a minor quirk of memory compared with Waugh's more extreme Pinfoldian experiences. However, the nature of Waugh's subconscious rewriting shows a novelist's mind at work. Waugh remembered the incident as a scene in which Sutro, framed by

'My memory plays me tricks. I was sure you were sick in the debating hall.'
Letter from Evelyn Waugh to John Sutro, 1963.

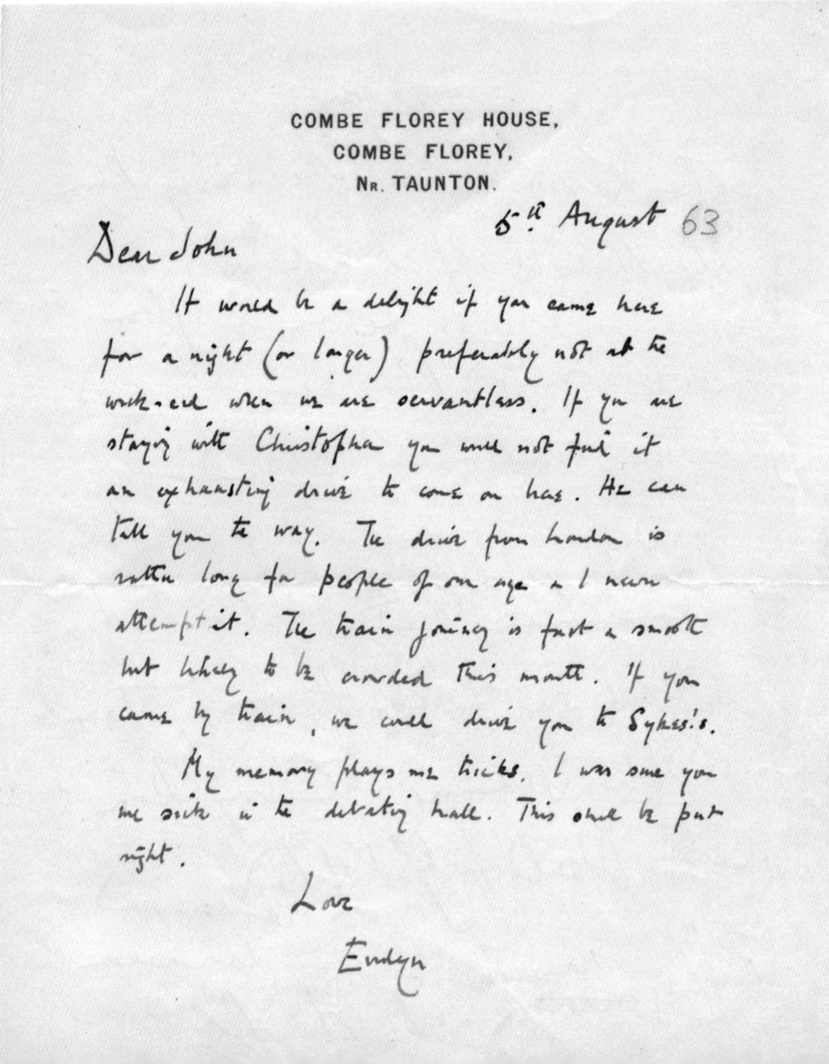

COMBE FLOREY HOUSE,
COMBE FLOREY,
Nr. TAUNTON.

5ᵗʰ August 63

Dear John

It would be a delight if you came here for a night (or longer) preferably not at the week-end when we are servantless. If you are staying with Christopher you will not find it an exhausting drive to come on here. He can tell you the way. The drive from London is rather long for people of our age & I never attempt it. The train journey is fast & smooth but likely to be crowded this month. If you came by train, we will drive you to Sykes's.

My memory plays me tricks. I was sure you were sick in the debating hall. This should be put right.

Love

Evelyn

the speaker's platform, vomits with a drama and decorum that perfectly illustrate his diffident nature and recalls Charles Ryder's observation of Sebastian's' parallel disgrace: 'There was ... a kind of insane and endearing orderliness about Sebastian's choice, in his extremity, of an open window.'[177] Despite Waugh's best efforts for accuracy and all its non-fiction credentials, Sutro's travelling vomit reveals the Oxford of *A Little Learning* to be no less an artist's impression than its *Brideshead* counterpart. The memory of an event is transformed in the novel, and the memory of the novel informs the later memoir.

In *Brideshead*, Charles Ryder evokes the recent past from the viewpoint of the 1940s, his present. His attitude, as the title of Book One suggests, is one of rapture and melancholy: he *was* in heaven, and can no longer be so. The narrator of *A Little Learning* shares some of Ryder's attitudes. For him, too, the past is an Arcadia and he observes that 'To have been born into a world of beauty, to die amid ugliness, is the common fate of all us exiles.'[178]

This narrator, however, no longer seems to belong to his contemporary world at all. Rather, he appears to have risen directly out of the lost Edwardian and Georgian landscapes he describes. Waugh addresses his audience, tongue only just in cheek,[179] as 'Gentle reader'[180] and, according to one representative reviewer, his 'vocabulary and syntax' convey an 'old-world air, like a well-dressed sexagenarian wearing spats'.[181] There is an element of camp in this narrative persona, and, given the book's autobiographical content, many 1960s commentators read this overt characterization as a deflection from the 'real' Waugh. 'In his dire way', V.S. Pritchett acidly observed, Waugh 'has done what he can do to pass himself off as a fossil'.[182]

But why, assuming we accept Pritchett's view, did Waugh feel the need to 'pass himself off' as anything? One possible answer is that, for Waugh, outward vaudeville was the prerequisite for inner privacy. The central importance of memory to that secret, protected inner self is expressed by *Brideshead*'s Ryder, who declares his memories to be synonymous with his life, 'for we possess nothing certainly except the past'. These memories, he adds, 'were always with me'.[183]

The companionship Ryder feels in his memories reflects Waugh's grounding of stable personal identity in permanence and continuity, which for him found their ideal form in the Catholic faith. During the writing of *A Little Learning* Waugh published an article in *The Spectator* which describes his recent attendance at a typical country Mass. The experience is nothing out of the ordinary, but nevertheless is at one with every Mass ever said and every Catholic soul. The familiar liturgy, spoken in a humble setting, has the power to unite all temporal moments in one shared sacrament:

> As the service proceeded in its familiar way I wondered how many of us wanted to see any change. ... The priest stood rather far away ... the language he spoke was not that of everyday use. This was the Mass for whose restoration the Elizabethan martyrs had gone to the scaffold. St Augustine, St Thomas à Becket, St Thomas More, Challoner and Newman would have been perfectly at their ease among us; were, in fact, present there with us.[184]

Waugh's article was prompted by the modernizing proposals of the Second Vatican Council, which it hoped would involve the congregation more actively in the liturgy of the Mass. Waugh was horrified by this break with tradition, and protested that the spiritual presence of the saints 'would not have been more palpable had we been making the responses aloud in the modern fashion'.[185]

For Waugh, the continuity of the Mass provided a connection to 'an English Catholic past, hazily and romantically conceived'.[186] In this he followed Father Martin D'Arcy, who had instructed him in Catholicism. Both Waugh and D'Arcy revered old Catholic families because, undeterred by the Reformation, they had kept the faith for hundreds of years. In this world-view, the Flytes of Brideshead Castle preserved a tradition more authentically English than upstart, sixteenth-century Protestantism and Charles's affection for the family is no simple proof of snobbery but rather a recognition that they are the human embodiment of the fundamentally unchanging nature of God. The making over of the Flytes' family home as an army billet is symbolic of a divorce from this permanence.

Despite this rift *Brideshead Revisited* takes comfort from the thought that, whatever might happen in the future, the past was secure. By the 1960s, however, there was reason to fear that even the past could not be possessed with any certainty. Public and private memory were under attack. What Vatican II did for the communal memory of the Catholic Church, amateur psychoanalysis (in Waugh's view) threatened for the individual.

Significantly, for an autobiography, *A Little Learning* makes repeated digs at psychological interpretation. For example, when Waugh declares that he loved his aunts' home because of a predilection for a mid-Victorian 'ethos', he suggests that 'psychologists would claim' rather that 'I now relish things of that period because they remind me of my aunts'. Similarly, when a childhood friend is told the brutal murder he witnessed was merely a 'bad dream', Waugh wonders if contemporary psychologists would approve.[187] The primary cause of this antagonism is also hinted at in the narrative. Just before Waugh began drafting the book he took part in a television interview, *Face to Face*, which he experienced as an impertinent and intrusive interrogation of his past. John Freeman, the programme's host, quizzed Waugh about his upbringing and schooling and seemed 'eager', according to Waugh, to 'disinter some hidden disaster or sorrow in my childhood'.[188] Waugh was having none of it. He responded first that his early life was 'lyrically happy' and then, after repeated questioning, 'idyllically happy'.[189] In *A Little Learning*, he describes these years as suffused with an 'even glow of pure happiness'. Such a blanket assertion need not mean that there was anything in particular to hide; it does, however, relay a determination to protect his memories from potentially damaging scrutiny. In Chapter 1 he describes the autobiography of a forebear as 'eschew[ing] personal revelation'.[190] The same was often said not just about Waugh's own autobiography but about his work in general.[191]

Some critics picked up a second diversionary tactic in *A Little Learning* which, in its theatricality, is closely allied to the 'carefully outmoded elegance'[192] of its narrative voice. In the book's final chapter, Sarel Eimerl observes,[193] the account of Waugh's attempted suicide comes hot on the heels of Captain Grimes's delighted exposition of sexual abuse:

> 'I confess I enjoyed myself greatly,' he said as we groused.
>   We regarded him incredulously. 'Enjoyed yourself, Grimes? What did you find to enjoy.'
>   'Knox minor,' he said with radiant simplicity. 'I felt the games a little too boisterous, so I took Knox minor away behind some rocks. I removed his boot and stocking, opened my trousers, put his dear little foot there and experienced a most satisfying emission.'[194]

Grimes was based on a teacher named Dick Young, and had previously appeared – exhibiting the same behaviour – in *Decline and Fall* (1928). For a contemporary audience, his disclosure in *A Little Learning* is both shocking and disturbing. For us, however, it is the fate of Knox minor which causes disquiet rather than, as was the case in the 1960s, the

language used to describe it. Waugh's contemporary audience was more
bothered by the sexual candour of the incident than its depiction of
the predatory behaviour of 1920s' schoolmasters. The *Sunday Times*, for
example, did not scruple to include Grimes's revelation in its serialization
of *A Little Learning* – but did cut the text after 'behind some rocks'.[195]
Waugh's fellow novelist and Oxford contemporary Anthony Powell had
also briefly encountered the teacher as a young man. Powell marvelled
at Young's innate novelistic quality, and rather than being disturbed by
him felt 'grateful to fate' that he had once been 'privileged' to meet
Grimes's original 'in the flesh'.[196]

Waugh's pious friend Katharine Asquith complained not about Knox
minor's welfare but that the text was 'uncivilised', and pined for a lost era
of reticence between
men and women.[197]
Waugh defended the
comedic value of the
confession to Asquith,
which he considered to
be due entirely to its
'grotesque details':

The real-life 'Captain
Grimes' boasted to Waugh
of his pederasty (illustration
to *Decline and Fall*,
Chapman & Hall, 1928).

here was a new, senior master … who had given no hint of his
sexual proclivities nor had any indication that any of us would
have any sympathy with them. He suddenly electrified us with an
unsought & unexpected confession told with complete aplomb.[198]

Eimerl was similarly unmoved by Grimes's victim but instead focused
on the shock and brutal hilarity of the incident, which in his view acted
as a smokescreen for the depth of despair that follows it. Eimerl saw the
contrast as a hallmark of Wavian style, in which 'there has always lurked,
outshone by the sparkle, signs of a sober melancholy'.[199]

In the denouement of *A Little Learning*, Waugh's life is narrated with
a mix of honesty and concealment. He refers more than once in this
final chapter to being at the end of his 'tether', but his suffering is made
absurd through both its pairing with the Captain Grimes episode and the
drowning attempt's thwarting by jellyfish. Waugh casts aspersions on his
own sincerity: 'Did I really intend to drown myself?'[200] he asks, just as a
few pages previously he dismisses his troubles at Oxford in a few lines:

It would be false to represent my undergraduate life as one of
uninterrupted mirth. There were quarrels and crapulosities and
transient bouts of the despair of adolescence.[201]

As Waugh matured, he was plagued by numerous bouts of despair
which were neither transient nor adolescent. Diverting attention from
them through disguise, absurdity and a forbidding exterior was to
become a distinguishing feature of his life and work.

City of Imagination

Though they differ slightly in narrative style, both *Brideshead Revisited* and *A Little Learning* describe the past in honeyed and glowing tones. However, in the years immediately following his departure from the city, Waugh composed Oxford using a quite different palette.

The gulf between idealized past and disappointing reality is encapsulated in two rival judgements made of Waugh's old haunt the Hypocrites Club, the first made in 1924 and the second in 1964. In the September following Waugh's disastrous viva, he travelled back to Oxford with Alastair Graham. It was a farewell trip, as Graham was due to sail out for Kenya in a few days' time. The boys spent their first night in the city 'discomfortably enough at 31 St Aldate's in clothes and on benches'. The next day, Waugh recorded that 'Everything was inexpressibly sordid; I hated 31 St Aldate's for its discomfort and its associations.'[202] By contrast, from the vantage point of 1964, Waugh remembered not so much the discomfort or sleaziness of the club but its symbolic importance as 'the source of friendships still warm today'.[203]

Without the benefit of hindsight, the young Waugh could not know that his Oxford acquaintances would remain friends. In *A Question of Upbringing* (1951), the first volume of *Dance to the Music of Time*, Anthony Powell broods on the abruptness with which student friendships could be severed once one party left the University. Powell's narrator accepts his broken bond with Stringham as 'the inevitability of circumstance' and the result of fast diverging experience. He reflects that often such connections could 'decay, quickly and silently, so that those concerned scarcely know how brittle, or how inflexible, the ties that bind them have become'.[204] Powell himself experienced this 'snapp[ing] ... of the links' numerous times, as by his third year seven of his closest associates had gone (or, more usually, been sent) down.[205] But while Powell and the *Upbringing* narrator remained in Oxford, Waugh was one of those to be cast out. Coupled with Graham's desertion to Africa, this felt like being cast out of the world.

The desolation of Waugh's first post-Oxford years is explored in 'The Balance: A Yarn of the Good Old Days of Broad Trousers and High Necked Jumpers'. This is the most experimental of all Waugh's works, and markedly more accomplished than his student writings. The narrative follows Adam Doure, an art-school student hopelessly in love with Imogen Quest, as he returns to his old university in search of someone to eat and get drunk with. He has a bottle of pills and a suicide note in his pocket. One by one his former friends make their excuses until Adam is forced to seek the dissolute and depressing company of Ernest Vaughan. Following an evening of weary and mechanical drinking, Adam takes an overdose but vomits up the pills overnight.

This fairly straightforward plot is complicated and fragmented in a number of directions which capitalize on Waugh's interest in early cinema and express Adam's profound dissociation and sense of detachment. The opening and closing sections of the narrative, for example, convey the impression that Adam is exiled from his own story: he is referenced by other characters in mildly disparaging terms but does not himself appear. These conversations take place during fashionable gatherings to which Adam is evidently not invited, and so also emphasize his isolation (the words 'alone' or 'solitude' occur in relation to Adam seven times during the text). Towards the end of the narrative, following his suicide attempt, Adam engages in a philosophical debate with his own reflection as it lies, breaking up, on the surface of an Oxford river.[206]

The most ambitious conceit of 'The Balance' is its suggestion that Adam's despair might not be 'real' at all but merely the motivation of an actor in an avant-garde film. Adam's rejection at the hands of Imogen and his Oxford friends are relayed as part of a screenplay, complete with sets, directions, captions and even an audience to comment on the action. His principal critics are Gladys and Ada, a 'cook and house-parlourmaid from a small house in Earls Court', who struggle to define the genre of the film:

> 'Go on. I say, Gladys, what sort of picture is this – is it comic?'
> The screen is almost completely dark as though the film has been greatly over-exposed. Fitful but brilliant illumination reveals a large crowd dancing, talking and eating.
> 'No, Ada – that's lightning. I dare say it's a desert storm. I see a picture like that the other day with Fred.' ...
> 'No, it isn't comic, Ada – it's Society.'
> 'Society's sometimes comic. You see.'[207]

Occasionally their commentary is joined by a young man with a 'Cambridge accent' who points out the film's failings in order to showcase his own superior knowledge.

The presence of these characters is a reminder that Waugh's student visits to the cinema constituted some of the rare occasions when 'Oxford' was not synonymous with 'University'; different social groups mixed in the auditorium and tried to make sense of one another. Ada and Gladys are clearly (if bluntly) representative of the working class and popular expectations of the film, the accepted genres for which were already fixed: romance, comedy, adventure and 'society'. Their attitudes are contrasted with self-consciously more 'cultured', high-art tastes of the young man from Cambridge. The two women's attempts to categorize the people they see on-screen speak to this social stratification: the beau monde, bohemian and 'bolshevist'[208] labels are all tried but found to be unequal to the narrative's unexpected course.

Ada and Gladys, like readers of 'The Balance', are confounded by the narratives they try to follow. The reader's first surprise is the very existence of Ada and Gladys, who wander into the cinema, and the story, one scene late. As such, they function as a radically unstable and unreliable frame text. The second surprise comes with the realization that, even as it belatedly establishes the cinema conceit, Waugh's narrative works to undermine it. In a note preceding this section of the narrative we are told that the 'conversations in the film are deduced by the experienced picture-goer from the gestures of the actors; only those parts which appear in capitals are actual "captions".' However, an omniscient narrator keeps intruding on this supposedly literal commentary with details which could not be 'deduced' by any viewer. For example, in Adam's art class apparently one picture 'will be better [than Adam's] at the end of the week', a fellow student criticizes his work using the (non-captioned) words that their instructor has just used to her, and the instructor and school secretary share 'a pathetic game of make-believe ... played endlessly ... in which they pretend that somewhere there is a code of rules which all must observe'.[209] This arch, ironical tone is developed further in *Decline and Fall* and *Vile Bodies*; given that this narrative is primarily concerned with the destabilization of Adam's identity, this parallel destabilization of its internal structure is unlikely to be an accident of authorial inexperience. Indeed, even within the film

Waugh's first novel *Decline and Fall* (Chapman & Hall, 1928), which he also illustrated, begins and ends in Oxford.

meaning mischievously splinters as soon as it is established; when the action moves to Oxford the scene shift is announced with an 'art caption' which first quotes Quiller Couch's 'Alma Mater' (as, too, would *A Little Learning*) before displaying the image of an ox, in a ford.[210]

Waugh struggled to find a publisher for his experimental story. Perhaps editors, like Gladys and Ada, found it difficult to 'place'. It was rejected by Leonard Woolf at the Hogarth Press and a number of other houses[211] before Evelyn's brother Alec included it in his 1926 anthology *Georgian Stories*.[212]

Waugh's first novel, *Decline and Fall*, appeared two years later. Like 'The Balance', it underwent rejection (by Duckworth, who had just

Hertford College group, June 1923. Waugh is fifth from right in the front row.

published Waugh's biography on D.G. Rossetti) before being picked up by Chapman & Hall.[213] *Decline and Fall* is very different in character to 'The Balance': its misfortunes are absurd rather than existential, and the plot's multiple about-turns (or risings and fallings) are contained in a circular structure which suffers no loose ends. Tonally, it has more in common with Waugh's student output than the later story, and translates the latter's structural unreliability into a more literal appetite for destruction.[214]

In the opening pages of *Decline and Fall* we find ourselves back, once again, in Oxford. This time people and places are lightly fictionalized: it is the night of the 'Bollinger' Club's annual dinner, and the Junior Dean and Domestic Bursar of 'Scone' College (modelled closely on Hertford) look on with growing delight as these eminent sons of 'English county families' smash up the rooms of the most unpopular students, break windows, drown a Matisse painting and – as a final 'treat' – deprive one Paul Pennyfeather of his trousers.[215] For this misfortune Pennyfeather is sent down on a charge of gross indecency, takes a job in a substandard public school, gets engaged to the mother of one of his pupils, is imprisoned for her crimes, released through her auspices and rejoins Scone posing as his own cousin less than a year later. Like Adam Doure and Charles Ryder, Paul shares some aspects of his author's biography. He goes to Oxford from an ecclesiastical school in the South Downs and, in contrast with the Bollinger, is conspicuously middle class.[216]

Paul's Oxford, like Adam's, is no Arcadia. We are introduced to Scone at a moment when the philistinic Bollinger Club is in full command, mounting a series of assaults on the property and persons of the more 'aesthetic' students. The 'Bollinger' is obviously a moniker for the Bullingdon Club, which appears under its own name in 'The Balance', various other Waugh short stories and *Brideshead Revisited*. In *Mad World*, Paula Byrne gives an enlightening summary of the Bullingdon in Waugh's day:

> The Bullingdon was a top-secret (all male, of course) dining club
> …. Then, as now, it drew its membership from the super rich. It
> was known then for champagne drinking, ritualised violence and
> a uniform that consisted of exquisite Oxford blue tailcoats offset
> with ivory silk lapel revers, brass monogrammed buttons, mustard
> waistcoat and sky blue bow tie. All members had to endure a
> humiliating initiation rite that included having their rooms trashed
> as champagne was binged upon and regurgitated.[217]

The 'baying' that Waugh attributes to the Bollinger connotes the 'awful screaming' that accompanied the Oxford's bullies' picking out of their next victim; they emitted exactly the same noise on a hunt, when the fox came into view.[218]

In *Decline and Fall* the Bollinger cavort with the tacit approval of the Junior Dean and Domestic Bursar, who, as the remainder of Scone has made itself scarce, are the sole representatives of College authority. The two men look forward to gathering the resultant penalties for bad behaviour (when College fines reach fifty pounds, we are told, a 'highly prized port' is brought up from the senior common room cellars), and predict the Bollinger's excesses with parental indulgence:

> 'Austen has a grand piano.'
>   'They'll enjoy smashing that.'[219]

The attitude of the Junior Dean and Domestic Bursar recalls Waugh's earlier 'Children's Corner' personae, and is echoed in the narrative voice as it remarks 'What an evening that had been!' and relates the 'lovely College meeting' that follows the blind.[220]

Waugh's romantic attachment to Oxford was formed before his student days. It re-emerges in his later works. In *A Little Learning* Waugh suggests that his two and a half years in the city provoked only 'small disillusionment'.[221] This claim, however, is challenged by the depiction of Oxford in *Decline and Fall*, and the narrative presents an interesting problem for those convinced of Waugh's essential snobbery. Culture is not produced at Scone College but destroyed;[222] destroyed, moreover, by the upper classes of which Waugh was apparently so adoringly uncritical. Paul Pennyfeather, explicitly described as 'someone of no importance',[223] takes the fall for the decimation and is sent down because he is not rich enough to be worth fining. This scenario neatly reverses the fates of Edward and Lord Poxe in 'Edward of Unique Achievement': Edward inadvertently frames Poxe for the murder of Mr Curtis, but in order to preserve his family's good name (which Poxe 'had always found ... of vast value' among tradesmen and dons) Poxe is let off with a thirteen-shilling fine.[224]

Laura Wade's fictitious Riot Club bears a striking resemblance to Oxford's notorious Bullingdon.

The 'comically venal'[225] college authorities and the Bollinger/Bullingdon Club are clearly the objects of Waugh's satire in these opening scenes. In recent years, the latter target has gained in currency: former prime minister David Cameron and foreign secretary Boris Johnson were members at the same time, and the club was both vilified and glamorized in the 2014 film *The Riot Club* (based on Laura Wade's grittier play *Posh*).[226] The *Guardian*'s film reviewer suggests that 'Waugh looms large in [the] text and setting' of *The Riot Club*.[227] She is referring, of course, to *Brideshead Revisited*, but her critique of the film also has implications for *Decline and Fall*. Although in neither *The Riot Club* nor Waugh's novels are aristocratic philistines offered up as role models, the implied criticism may not wholly expunge a grudging admiration of their audacity.[228]

If so, however, in Waugh's narratives at least admiration is not predicated on the social status of the wrongdoers. It applies equally to all *Decline and Fall*'s spectacular anti-heroes, regardless of class. For example, in his introduction to the novel, Frank Kermode explains how the character of Captain Grimes is built up through successive manuscript drafts to occupy his position among 'the immortals'. In reality, Waugh had quickly tired of the pederastic schoolteacher Dick Young, on whom Grimes was based. Kermode points out that Young had none of Grimes's glory or pathos, and despite his sinister behaviour the latter manages to command a readerly sympathy.[229] Socially, Grimes is aligned with Paul in the novel: not an aristocrat but a gentleman.

Decline and Fall's impressive cast of villains and eccentrics also have the effect of pushing Paul, our supposed protagonist, into the background. Towards the close of the novel the architect Otto Silenus (a caricature

of famed modernist designer Le Corbusier) divides people into two categories: 'dynamic' and 'static'. Paul is definitively 'static'.[230] He is thrown onto fortune's crazy wheel by the actions of the Bollinger Club, and henceforth a series of events happen *to* him. He makes almost nothing happen on his own. As such, he is the literary equivalent

Otto Silenus categorizes people as 'dynamic' or 'static' (Waugh's illustration to *Decline and Fall*, Chapman & Hall, 1928).

of the marionettes who illustrate Waugh's cover design for *Cherwell*,[231] most content when someone else is pulling his strings.

It is only right that Paul ends his misadventures back where he started. The only difference is that he is now posing at Scone College as his own cousin and, given his lack of interiority, it is arguable whether that makes any difference beyond his newly adopted 'heavy cavalry moustache'. Oxford is following exactly the same course as it was before Paul's anomalous year, a circumstance emphasized by the epilogue's repetition of numerous phrases and situations from the prelude. It is, once again, the annual Bollinger dinner, the source of 'confused roaring and breaking of glass';[232] Paul has attended a second interesting paper on Polish plebiscites, and is in 'his third year of uneventful residence'. A static man is returned to a cyclical environment, which allots roles to players who occupy them for a while before handing over, willingly or otherwise, to the next incumbent. Thus is Paul able to continue his disrupted life under the guise of his own cousin. We have come full circle.

Waugh was not the only writer to notice the split in Oxford's personality between great age and an eternal youth, serviced by interchangeable youths. The combination was unsettling for his friend Henry Yorke, later known as Henry Green, who went up to the University the term after Waugh went down. The tyranny of Oxford's three-year cycle weighed heavy on Green, who observed that young dons began 'by making friends for the first nine years of [their] time and then, when [they have] found three lots of friends drop out [begin] to have had enough'. As for the undergraduates, the constant ringing of church and chapel bells reminded them of every minute gone and engendered the foreboding 'that it will soon be too late' – for their generation at least.[233] In Waugh's case, even this small ration of time was cut short and his Oxford years remained forever unfinished.

The structure of Waugh's first novel, which mirrors the rhythm of the university he had just been obliged to leave, is repeated and reversed in his last book. In *A Little Learning* this circularity is partly the result of accident. Waugh intended to continue the narrative up to his thirtieth birthday but,[234] as it is, the final chapter sees him returning to boarding school. He is now ineffectual master instead of disaffected pupil; the essential loneliness and unpopularity remain. So it is that in Waugh's revised scheme, the last pages of *A Little Learning* look forward – and back – to the genesis of *Decline and Fall*. We are introduced to Hamish/Alastair's 'high-tempered, possessive, jolly and erratic' mother as the inspiration for the stridently rude Lady Circumference, and encounter Captain Grimes in Waugh's hilarious yet unhappy staffroom, in the school which he would 'lavishly' embellish to do service as Llanabba Castle.[235] The sacrosanct Oxford of Waugh's youth sits regally between these twin ordeals.

The strange ways in which time behaved in Evelyn Waugh's Oxford also served to set the city apart. In *A Little Learning* the author tells us that in the 1920s the city represented 'a single lustrum' in which 'we lived and spoke very much as our predecessors had done ten years before'.[236] 'Lustrum' is right. Despite the disagreement between the satirized city of Waugh's early writings and its later, more idealized forms, in every case Oxford appears to live its own existence, occasionally intersecting with the outside world, but remaining distinct from and indifferent to it.

Oxford's oddly hermetic quality, closely allied to its timelessness, is also conveyed both thematically and structurally in Waugh's writings. Charles Ryder, for example, preserves Oxford as an unassailable memory and the repository of 'centuries of youth', while in 'The Balance' the sections of the story taking place in the city are part of a film which ends with Adam's attempted suicide. In *Decline and Fall* the cyclical life of Scone College is separated from the main narrative as Prologue and Epilogue.

When Waugh went up to Oxford at the age of eighteen, his mind was 'aglow with literary associations' and he spent his time in the city building on this well-formed 'preconception of the place'.[237] Over the years he would make his own contribution to this literary Oxford, even to redefine the vision that had first inspired him. In turn, his student memories and experiences would nourish his writing from first to last. There is a sense, then, in which for Waugh Oxford was always as much a city of imagination as it was objective reality. Such a place might be revisited in memory, but never in fact; an 'enclosed and enchanted garden', as Charles Ryder had it, 'which was somewhere, not overlooked by any window, in the heart of that grey city'.[238]

The Oxford of Waugh's literature is always necessarily distorted, and entirely self-sufficient. Its buildings, people and places cannot provide a 'key' that unlocks the writings for us, mapping this character onto that real-life friend or this student incident onto that crucial plot device, but exist in dialogue with them. Reading Waugh's life and works through his experiences in Oxford forges new connections between real and imagined topographies, uncovers new meanings in overlooked corners, and illuminates pure coincidences which shed new light on Waugh's city, his life and his work.

Like Carroll's Wonderland, Waugh's Oxford was a closed, enchanted world.

*Exploring
Waugh's
Oxford*

Hertford College

In the front row of Hertford College's group photograph for June 1923 (p. 68), a young man sits hunched and cross-legged. He is not smiling. He is short, and perhaps being pushed upfront is an unpleasant reminder of the fact. Or perhaps his neighbours, knees falling out to their sides, are encroaching too much on his personal space.

It is not surprising that Evelyn Waugh looks unhappy in this photograph. What is surprising is that he bothered to turn up for it at all. By Waugh's second year, his disdain for his college was entrenched with a vehemence that would allow for only very small concessions.

In *A Little Learning* Waugh recalls his school headmaster's diplomatic, if grammatically infelicitous, assessment of Hertford as 'a very rising college'. 'If I can believe my children,' Waugh continues, 'it has not yet risen to a higher position than it enjoyed in my time.'Before the book was published, this was phrased even more rudely as 'I gather from my children that it has sunk.'[1] But Waugh evidently thought better of that, and expunged the phrase from his typescript. He was not, after all, entirely devoid of gratitude for Hertford.One day in 1945, for example, when Waugh found himself unexpectedly lunchless in Oxford, the College was the only place in the city that would give him a decent meal. He was greeted warmly, and the porter 'offered to return my Shakespeare which I lost 20 years ago and have often thought of'.[2]

The most iconic features of Hertford were less than fifty years old when Waugh was up. Although there has been some kind of school there since the 1280s, the College has only existed in its current form since 1874.[3] That was the year when large donations from Thomas Charles Baring, 'staunch Conservative and strong Churchman', re-endowed the site and led to its considerable expansion.[4] The remodelling was undertaken by Sir Thomas Jackson R.A. (1835–1924), whose eclectic, Gothic style had the epithet 'Anglo-Jackson'.[5] Hertford's chapel and hall, as well as the famous 'Bridge of Sighs', are all Jackson's work.[6]

Waugh was not impressed. For him, the 'Bridge of Sighs' was merely a conduit from the old part of the college to its modern bathrooms.[7] And when in 1930 Waugh wrote to the Oxford Preservation Trust, suggesting the 'judicious destruction' of many buildings in order to transform 'a comparatively ugly city [into] a comparatively beautiful one', the 'whole of Hertford' was on his hit list.[8]

In his third term Waugh moved into a ground-floor room at Hertford, facing out over the front quad.[9] In *Brideshead Revisited* Charles Ryder is housed in the same location, thereby enabling Sebastian Flyte to introduce himself by vomiting in through the window. Sebastian makes amends for this lapse in etiquette by filling Charles's rooms with flowers and inviting him to lunch among the splendours of Christ Church.[10] In Julian Jarrold's film of the novel, Charles is belittled at this lunch. Sebastian's friend, Boy Mulcaster, asks him what school he went to: Harrow, Winchester, Rugby or, God forbid, Charterhouse:

> Charles: You wouldn't have heard of it.
> Boy: Oh.
> Sebastian: There are other schools, you know, Boy.
> Boy: Well yes, I suppose there *must* be.[11]

Waugh has often been dismissed as a snob, and *Brideshead Revisited* as a snobbish book, but the film version highlights something a little more nuanced. Charles is middle class, like Waugh, but does not pretend to be someone he is not – rather, he resents being looked down upon for who he is. This was a sensitive point for Waugh too, who throughout his life was plagued by a sense of social inferiority. Snubs like this cut close to the bone. Boy's sneer has its biographical counterpart in remarks such as those made by Conrad Russell, a rival for the affections of Waugh's close friend Diana Cooper. Russell condemned Waugh as 'not quite a gentleman, not quite, not quite.'[12]

Waugh, educated at a second-choice public school, son of a publisher who revelled in his middle-classness,[13] was already nursing a suspicion of being 'not quite' when he went up to university. It was a feeling that his alma mater, with all its arriviste grandeur, did little to dispel. Perhaps Waugh had too much in common with Hertford for it ever to be truly home.

The New Theatre

On 13 February 1886, in George Street, a young Arthur Waugh sat in the packed auditorium of a newly built theatre. The walls still smelled of paint. It was the premiere of the Oxford University Dramatic Society's first ever play, *Twelfth Night*; anticipation was high, and the audience 'red-hot with enthusiasm'. They were mostly rewarded – Viola was, apparently, below par – and the production launched a new era in Oxford drama.[14]

Evelyn's father was not a very remarkable undergraduate. He was more interested in the stage than his studies and, according to Evelyn, the enthusiasm cost him the chance of a good degree.[15] Arthur took advantage of the newly formed OUDS to visit the theatre as often as he could, where he enjoyed 'simple, natural, cup-and-saucer' comedies by largely forgotten playwrights.[16]

Acting was the only passion Arthur shared with his bullying father, Dr Alexander Waugh, but he did not join OUDS. According to Evelyn, this was due to his father's ill health; but Arthur has a sadder explanation. In his autobiography, he writes that he 'never joined ... partly because nobody asked me' and partly because he feared the club would be too expensive.[17] Arthur, however, was not totally out of the limelight. He acted during the vacations and, in his final year, pulled off the considerable feat of writing a whole play script in one sitting, 'snatching a sandwich lunch between sentences'. The play was a spoof of the OUDS' recent *Julius Caesar*, entitled *Julius Seesawcer, Or, A Storm in a Tea-cup*. It was cast and rehearsed in a fortnight, and performed at the Holywell Music Room on Saturday, 16 March 1889.[18]

Evelyn did not join OUDS either, but he did act in a few of Terence Greenidge's silent films, and in the summer of 1924, just after he went down, he wrote *The Scarlet Woman* for his friend. In this 'ecclesiastical melodrama', the Dean of Balliol (Evelyn) seduces the Prince of Wales (Terence's brother John) to Catholicism and plans a massacre of the country's leading Protestants. He is thwarted by a cabaret dancer, played by the film star Elsa Lanchester in her first screen role.[19] *The Scarlet Woman* also starred Alec Waugh and Gyles Isham, who *was* in OUDS and went on to a successful acting career.

The Scarlet Woman gave Arthur the chance to relive his theatrical youth. The screenplay was filmed on Hampstead Heath and in his own back garden at Underhill.[20] Evelyn had just moved back into the family home, and the fun of the venture eased some of the tension between father and son. In *A Little Learning*, Evelyn remembers how Arthur 'delighted to find the cast at his table and when the film was shown him took particular satisfaction in recognising his own possessions. "That's my chair" ... "Take care you don't break that decanter."'[21] This reminiscence is warm enough, but it also carries a whiff of indulgence. Seen through Evelyn's eyes, there is something not quite dignified in Arthur's response.

When Evelyn came to write *Vile Bodies*, he included a subplot in which Nina Blount's eccentric father opens up his country house to a film crew. Colonel Blount is keen to get in front of the cameras, and the company humour him with bit parts in the crowd scenes. '"He was crazy to be allowed to come on"', says one of the actors, '"and as he's letting us the house dirt cheap Isaacs [the director] said he might. I don't believe he's ever been so happy in his life."'[22] When the producer runs into financial difficulties the Colonel, desperate for the film to be a success, buys it from him. Although Arthur Waugh did not take a role in *The Scarlet Woman,* these scenes in *Vile Bodies* may have made uncomfortable reading. Blount is not an unsympathetic character, but he is silly and deluded.

The theatre party might not have been as much fun for Evelyn as it was for his father. As a young man, he was wary of bringing friends back to Underhill lest Arthur poached them for himself.[23] The same possessiveness flares in *Brideshead Revisited*'s Sebastian when Charles shows an interest in his family: '"All my life they've been taking things away from me. If they once got hold of you with their charm, they'd make you their friend not mine, and I won't let them."'[24]

Insulting Arthur was one way for Evelyn to mark his territory, to draw a line between what belonged to his father and what to him. In some directions this was simple enough; in terms of temperament and priorities, Arthur and Evelyn were wildly at odds. But when it came to theatricals, the distinction was less clear. As a teenager, Evelyn invited a friend to Underhill whose opinion of Arthur could apply equally to father or son: 'Charming, entirely charming, and acting all the time.'[25]

Hall Brothers

When Waugh was at Oxford, all dapper undergraduates bought their suits from Hall Bros. The tailors were a city institution, and in the 1920s traded from a mock-Tudor building, replete with Elizabeth I's coat of arms, at 94 Magpie Lane.[26]

Waugh was always fine-tuned to the look of things, and the Hall Bros style was familiar to him before he even knew of the tailors' existence. To begin with, as he writes in *A Little Learning*, Waugh associated this fashion with an older generation, personified in his calligraphy tutor Francis Crease, whose 'dress was the rural-aesthetic of the period, soft tweeds, cloaks, silk shirts and ties of the kind which later became familiar to me at Hall Bros in the High at Oxford'. Dr Counsell or 'Doggins', senior member of the Railway Club, also wore Hall Bros signature 'rough silk shirts and ties'.[27]

In the vibrant post-war period, however, Hall Bros adapted to meet the changing tastes of its youthful clientele. In the 1920s they became the city's foremost purveyor of 'Oxford bags', very wide trousers first popularized by Waugh's friend Harold Acton.[28] Oxford bags really took off after Waugh had left, but they belonged firmly to a period when he still thought, talked and dressed like an undergraduate and became one of those – as he put it – 'who cannot at once sever the cord uniting them to the university and haunt it for years to come'.[29] Like his student friends, Waugh teamed his bags with a high- or 'turtle'-neck jumper, which, he observed in November 1924, was 'rather becoming and most convenient for lechery because it dispenses with all unromantic gadgets like studs and ties. It also hides the boils with which most of the young men seem to have encrusted their necks.'[30] One of his first short stories to be published outside Oxford was subtitled in honour of this forgiving get-up: 'The Balance: A Yarn of the Good Old Days of Broad Trousers and High Necked Jumpers' (1926).

Waugh's appreciation of the turtleneck jumper was typical of his pragmatic approach to fashion at the time. On Christmas Day 1924, he resolved to 'try and grow a moustache because I cannot afford any new clothes for several years and I want to see some change in myself. Also if I am to be a school master it will help to impress the urchins with my age.'[31] As his financial situation eased, however, Waugh raised his sartorial ambitions. His brother Alec introduced him to Anderson Sheppard of London's Savile Row,[32] whose suits made him feel, for the first time, not 'the worst dressed person in every room'.[33] Being well turned out satisfied more than just Waugh's vanity. For a man of his relatively humble origins, the cut of a seam could be the difference between social acceptance and rejection.

Despite his London-bought sophistication, Waugh parted from his first tailors with regret. He had his last suit from Hall Bros in February 1926,[34] and settled his many Oxford debts later in the year. As he made his way from creditor to creditor, pocketbook in hand, he thought that Hall Bros had 'some real personal feeling' for him, and was the only shop sorry to see him go.[35]

Waugh cut an increasingly distinctive figure as he grew older, choosing ever louder and bolder clothing that became positively eccentric. He had gone from wanting to look the part to playing a part, from couture to costume. He was well aware of the process, explaining in his semi-autobiographical novel *The Ordeal of Gilbert Pinfold* that he caricatured himself as a 'protective disguise ... the price he paid for privacy'. It was a high price. Pinfold grew so ill-at-ease in company that when he

> ceased to be alone, when he swung into his club or stumped up the nursery stairs, he left half of himself behind and the other half swelled to fill its place. He offered the world a front of pomposity mitigated by indiscretion, that was as hard, bright and antiquated as a cuirass.[36]

The older Waugh both dressed and behaved with a flamboyancy that screened his deepening conviction that he was no longer fit for the society he'd once craved. His conversation, he felt, had been stripped of its charm until only boredom and insult remained. His clothing was a defence against both: if he sounded dull, he would never look it. And if he stung, then at least he'd had the decency to put on warning stripes.

New College

On a warm and windy Saturday in June 1923[37] the Oxford University Dramatic Society opened its production of *The Rhesus* in New College gardens. It was performed in the original Greek,[38] and boasted a handsome programme: a bold woodcut of Rhesus' mother, one of the nine muses, holding up her son's slain body (p. 30). The programme was designed by Evelyn Waugh.[39]

To a younger Waugh, Oxford was synonymous with New College. He had known it from childhood as his father's alma mater, and as the time approached for Evelyn to apply for his University scholarship Arthur took him on a visit there. It was Waugh's first experience of the College as a familial space. Arthur caught up on gossip with the College servants, who greeted them warmly and showed Evelyn his father's old rooms.[40] Arthur regaled Evelyn with 'disreputable stories of his time' and the son left the city enchanted. 'I have never seen anything so beautiful', he recorded in his diary.[41]

Evelyn was part of the fifth generation of Waughs to attend Oxford.[42] Arthur wanted him to follow even closer in his footsteps and put his name down for New College,[43] but in the event he ended up round the corner, at Hertford. Depending on the time of day he might literally be in the shadow of the older, grander building. Evelyn's brother Alec had been obliged to leave school before scholarship time came round, and then went straight into the army. Thus Oxford was one thing Arthur and Evelyn, as opposed to Arthur and Alec, had in common – but it did not bond them. Rather, Evelyn's reckless behaviour at Oxford embarrassed Arthur and soured his own memories of his student years.[44] And, ironically, Waugh junior repeated his father's achievements in the only area of which neither man was proud. Arthur went down with a double third in Mods and Greats; Evelyn left without a degree at all.

Arthur and Evelyn never got on, and their strained dynamic permeates Waugh's writing from first to last. Works as varied as *A Handful of Dust*, *Brideshead Revisited* and the *Sword of Honour* trilogy are kindred in their representations of paternal or pseudo-paternal relationships, which range from the abductive and demonic to the gentle and mutually protective.

In Waugh's early and mid-career works, this dynamic takes the form of son or 'son' as an unwilling or begrudged guest in his father's house. In *A Handful of Dust*, for example, Tony Last is first cured then held captive in rural South America by Mr Todd, literal father to a whole village of illegitimate children. Bizarrely, Tony is condemned to read the complete works of Dickens on perpetual rotation to his illiterate gaoler[45] – a fate which owes much to the particular tensions of the Waugh family home. In the evenings, Arthur liked to read aloud to his family from the comfort of his book-room. As a young man forced back by penury to Underhill, Waugh found these nightly performances, which often included Dickens readings, unendurable.[46]

Like Tony Last, Charles Ryder is also a kind of captive, obliged by his own profligacy to spend long periods at home. Ryder senior knows Charles would prefer to be elsewhere, but that he has spent all his allowance during the University term and so cannot afford to travel or eat out. As a punishment, we assume, for his son's poor budgeting, Ryder senior goes out of his way to make life uncomfortable for Charles. He invites deliberately boring people to dinner, and when his son brings home a friend of his own, old Mr Ryder plays a 'one-sided parlour game' in which he affects to believe their guest is American.[47]

A Handful of Dust and *Brideshead Revisited* express the frustration of men unable to claim their freedom from odious father figures. As such, their struggles parallel not only Waugh's irritation at finding himself materially bound to the family home but also the burden he felt of being just one more member of a literary dynasty and, in his student years, just one more Waugh at Oxford. As a publisher and critic (and father) Arthur made it his business to nurture young talent, and as a result the family book-room had a whole shelf of volumes that bore grateful dedications to him.[48] A teenage Evelyn mocked these panegyrics in a dedication written to himself, in which he anticipates that his upbringing among books and literary chatter will count against his own efforts: 'Another of these precocious Waughs,' they will say, "one more nursery novel".' But, he adds defiantly, 'So be it'.[49]

Some years later, in Waugh's unfinished novel *Work Suspended*, a son breaks free in dramatic and bleakly comic fashion. In Chapter 1, John Plant's needlingly malevolent father (like Arthur Waugh, a Victorian man with middlebrow sensibilities) is killed in a car accident.[50] By now, however, Evelyn had not only gained his independence from Arthur but also succeeded in, as he saw it, bettering his achievements. He was no longer threatened by the object lesson of Arthur's supposed mediocrity, and for his part Arthur had less to disapprove of in his son. And then, not long after *Work Suspended* was first published, Arthur Waugh died.[51] Both factors contributed to the much more amenable, principled and unworldly father figure of Gervase Crouchback in the *Sword of Honour* series.

There was one further reason for Evelyn's late-realized benevolence. Their shared experience of Oxford had failed to bring them together, but the demands of fatherhood almost succeeded in bridging the gulf. Once Waugh became a father himself, he began to see Arthur in a different light. As his family grew he measured his paternal performance against his forebears' and observed that, while he was worse company to his own children than Arthur had been to him, he was at least kinder than his sadistic grandfather.[52] The realization was crystallized in his diary:

'Those who most reprobate and ridicule their fathers ... were not fathers themselves.'[53]

The Hypocrites Club

In December 1922 Waugh's school friend Tom Driberg went to Oxford to sit his scholarship exams. When Waugh sat his the year before, he had been well hosted by Lancing old boys. Now, he returned the favour for Tom by taking him to the Hypocrites Club.

Opinion differs about where exactly the Hypocrites was, but all agree that this noisy, smelly and short-lived establishment was located above a bicycle shop somewhere down the less salubrious end of St Aldate's.[54]

Waugh's own diary suggests number 31. Selina Hastings implies that the club took its name from its Pindarian motto – 'water is best'[55] – but a passage in Driberg's memoir *Ruling Passions* suggests a more provocative origin:

> The usual shallow sneer at homosexuals in any sort of public life … is that they are 'hypocrites'. Except in the sense that the Greek word 'hypocrite' means 'actor', and that, especially in an intolerant society, all of us have to do a certain amount of … role-playing, the charge is false.[56]

Waugh knew Driberg would not be shocked by the Hypocrites. His friend was confident in his sexuality, and had been sexually active – if not hyperactive – since early puberty. At the club, Driberg found a boy to dance with while Waugh 'rolled on a sofa' with another willing partner, their 'tongues licking each other's tonsils'.[57]

Waugh did not shy away from the Hypocrites' homosexual character. His autobiography was, however, less candid than Driberg's about his own participation in this aspect of its culture. There are pragmatic reasons for this. In England, homosexuality was decriminalized only in 1967;[58] *A Little Learning* was published just before, and *Ruling Passions* ten years after, this watershed. As such, it is hardly surprising that no one still living and appearing under their real name is identified as gay in Waugh's autobiography, or that Waugh gently euphemizes his own boyfriends as 'friend[s] of my heart'.[59]

Driberg, however, had an additional explanation for Waugh's reticence. According to him, his friend did not just have a 'homosexual phase'[60] at Oxford but was a closet bisexual, and spent the majority of his life repressing the fact. He even suggests that Waugh's mental breakdown in the 1950s was the result of this 'protective … role-playing'.[61]

Driberg assigns bisexuality to Waugh and presents him with only two options: to own that bisexuality openly, or to suffer the psychic damage of its repression. But books such as *Brideshead Revisited* explore sexuality in softer tones. Charles and Sebastian are Waugh's most famous same-sex couple, and much paper has been expended on whether or not they are involved in a fully physical sexual relationship.[62] Quite possibly, these either/or arguments are missing the point. There is no doubt that the boys love one another; the question is whether that love can, will or should last. For Lord Marchmain's mistress Cara, it is a question of innocence and experience, romance and wisdom:

> 'I think you are very fond of Sebastian,' she said.
> 'Why, certainly.'
> 'I know of these romantic friendships of the English and the Germans. They are not Latin. I think they are very good if they do not go on too long.'
> She was so composed and matter-of-fact that I could not take her amiss, but I failed to find an answer ...
> 'It is a kind of love that comes to children before they know its meaning. In England it comes when you are almost men; I think I like that. It is better to have that kind of love for another boy than for a girl.'[63]

Charles insists that his relationship with Sebastian is the 'forerunner'[64] to a more mature love for his sister, Julia, but the declaration rings hollow. It is hard for a reader to escape the impression that Charles's second, heterosexual love is a pale imitation of his first, homosexual one.

It is only a matter of time, perhaps, before someone writes an alternative *Brideshead Revisited* in which Charles and Sebastian stay together. The same could even be done for Waugh himself. Had Waugh lived in a different time, he might have chosen to disappear into Wales along with Alastair Graham. But, then again, he might not. Whilst writing *A Little*

Learning Waugh was in touch with the biographer Hugh Heckstall-Smith, who dismissed the concept of '100 per cent homosexual[ity]' as a 'pipe dream'. Instead, there might be any number of people who had 'latent homosexuality' in their 'make-up'.[65] Such thinking provides an alternative to Driberg's notion of a 'true nature' that must either be accepted or concealed.[66] Waugh loved men and women at different times in his life, but that did not necessarily make him heterosexual, homosexual or even bisexual. For Waugh, product of the early twentieth century, to be 'homosexual' meant to embrace a particular lifestyle with which his sympathy was short-lived, and he was comfortable to express attraction to individual men without 'identifying' as gay. He was just as comfortable to marry a woman and live a full life with her.

Waugh liked his meanings fixed and his world ordered. His fluid sexuality, however, evaded such easy definition.

Balliol College

As soon as Waugh ventured beyond Hertford's gates, he found himself in Balliol. He thought the architecture 'dismal' and the facilities bleak,[67] but despite these outward deficiencies the College had a sparkle Waugh thought sorely lacking in his own. There is a sense in which Balliol, and not Hertford, was Waugh's true alma mater. It was Balliol that he praised in *A Little Learning* and in Balliol that he spent his last night at the University, drinking to excess before being lowered out of a window by Lord Balfour[68] to climb across the garden of All Souls and back into Hertford unseen.[69] But to one member of the College, Waugh was a very unwelcome adopted son.

Balliol was home to many of Waugh's best friends. Alfred Duggan, a rich and affable alcoholic, who later became a successful historical novelist, resembled Waugh in his taste for exiting rooms by their windows. In Duggan's case, this enabled him to sneak out of the college and into a waiting car, ready to chauffeur him up to London for the night. Duggan's behaviour would have sent many an undergraduate down, but luckily his stepfather, Lord Curzon, was Chancellor of the University.[70] Graham Greene was also a Balliol man. He and Waugh would later be friends, but whilst at Oxford Greene kept to a set of (in his words) 'boisterous heterosexuals' who did not mix well with Waugh's Hypocrites and Aesthetes.[71] Two more men, Christopher Hollis and Richard Pares, enjoyed the particular attention of the college dean.

As dean of Balliol, Francis Fortescue ('Sligger') Urquhart was responsible for what was then considered Oxford's most prestigious college.[72] He took the task seriously, and was constantly on the lookout for exceptional scholars, whom he would absorb into his 'sober salon'[73] and take on vacation reading parties to his 'chalet on the foothills of Mont Blanc'. Sligger was also Oxford's first Roman Catholic don since the Reformation,[74] and was as much concerned with the moral welfare of his charges as with their intellectual development. Evelyn Waugh and the Hypocrites Club were a menace to both.

Richard Pares was never much of a drinker, and even in the depths of his affair with Waugh he did not forget his vocation. As the conflicting demands of their lifestyles threatened the relationship, Sligger took his chance and guided Pares back to academia.[75]

Waugh could later admit that it was not Sligger's machinations but drink which drove him and Pares apart.[76] At the time, however, it was less painful to blame the dean and Waugh persecuted him with a ferocity surpassed only by his hatred for Cruttwell. One evening, he and Christopher Hollis positioned themselves under Urquhart's windows and caroused, to the tune of 'Here We Go Gathering Nuts in May', 'The Dean of Balliol lies with men!'[77]

Waugh also granted Sligger an honour denied Cruttwell when, in 1924, he portrayed him on screen. In *The Scarlet Woman*, Waugh satirized Urquhart's religion and his practice of singling out talented young men to create a screenplay in which the dean of Balliol attempts to convert the entire country to Catholicism by manipulating the Prince of Wales. According to Terence Greenidge, the film's director, Waugh's impersonation of Sligger was 'suberb'; '[w]e did not know of the Marx brothers … but by telepathy (?) Evelyn drew enormously on Harpo Marx'.[78] It was an outrageously camp performance. Waugh, staring out possessively from under a badly fitting blonde wig, cannot keep his hands off the prince and sulks when his influence is eclipsed.[79] It bore no resemblance at all to the Urquhart Anthony Powell (another Balliol man) was later to describe as 'hesitant in manner, conversationally inhibited, never pontificating about public affairs, nor addicted more than most dons to the habit of intrigue'.[80]

Greenidge noted the irony that, given the film's depiction of an alcoholic pope and pederast don, many of its cast either were or soon became Catholics: '[b]ut I am uncertain of the moral of this!'[81] Whatever the link between the mocking and embracing of Catholicism, once Waugh shared a religion with Urquhart, his vendetta lost its force.

While he vilified Cruttwell into his last days, in *A Little Learning* Waugh describes Urquhart's fostering of Pares as a rescue and pays tribute to his first love's academic success.[82]

During the writing of *A Little Learning* Waugh contacted his Oxford friend Lord Clonmore, another Catholic convert, requesting permission to use his name in the memoir. Clonmore agreed, but took the opportunity to admonish Waugh for his youthful Sligger-baiting. 'As regards [that good man Sligger],' he wrote, 'I always think you & Chris [Hollis] broke his heart & killed him'.[83] If so, it was a slow death. Urquhart died in 1934, in his mid-sixties, ten years after Waugh went down. And as for breaking his heart, while a mature Waugh might have felt regret, his student self would merely have shrugged. Urquhart had already broken his.

The Junk Shop

Some time in 1922, 1923 or possibly 1924 a twitchy young man with nail-bitten fingers went into a junk shop in Walton Street and purchased a stuffed dog (breed and condition unknown). Later, he and a friend abandoned the unfortunate creature in their college quad. It was left out as bait for one C.R.M.F. Cruttwell, late of the Western Front and now History tutor at Hertford.

At least that's how Waugh remembered things. According to him, Terence Greenidge had a genius for bestowing unwanted epithets on his acquaintances. 'Hotlunch' was Hugh Molson, who always complained about midday bread and cheese; 'Baldhead who writes for the papers' was Waugh's brother Alec. But while there was truth in these monikers, Waugh also held Terence responsible for the rumour that Captain Cruttwell was indecently fond of dogs. The friends would bark under his window at night, [84] and belt out a song that Waugh, being Waugh, had composed in his honour:

Cruttwell dog, Cruttwell dog, where have you been?
I've been to Hertford to lie with the Dean.
Cruttwell dog, Cruttwell dog what did you there?
I bit off his penis and pubic hair.[85]

Terence was a strange boy, prone to obsessive fads and kleptomania. He was certainly imaginative to impute bestiality to Cruttwell, but the venom of the attack was all Waugh's. Waugh hated Cruttwell, and the stuffed-dog allurement was only the first in a lifelong series of creative insults. Throughout his writing career, Waugh would christen a string of sad, mad and bad characters 'Cruttwell': *Decline and Fall*'s Toby Cruttwell is a violent criminal, *Scoop!*'s General Cruttwell presides over a 'waterless and indefensible' World War I camp and sells William Boot useless expedition supplies, and *Black Mischief*'s 'silly' Captain Cruttwell is an afterthought dinner guest of Lady Seal. The insane Mr Loveday of 'Mr Loveday's Little Outing' was originally called Mr Crutwell,[86] Tom Kent-Cumberland of 'Winner Takes All' is strong-armed into marriage with the unhappy Gladys Cruttwell and 'An Englishman's Home' features the ineffectual accountant 'poor Mr Cruttwell'. Meanwhile the real Cruttwell dreaded the publication of every new Waugh title, wondering what appalling creation would, this time, bear his name.

Things had started off well enough. When Waugh won his scholarship to Hertford, Cruttwell wrote him a warm letter of congratulation. In person, however, they catastrophically failed to hit it off. In *A Little Learning*, Waugh describes Cruttwell in grotesque detail:

Cruttwell's appearance was not prepossessing. He was tall, almost loutish, with the face of a petulant baby. He smoked a pipe which was usually attached to his blubber-lips by a thread of slime. As he removed the stem, waving it to emphasise his indistinct speech, this glittering connection extended until finally it broke leaving a

dribble on his chin. When he spoke to me I found myself so dis-
tracted by the speculation of how far this line could be attenuated
that I was often inattentive to his words.[87]

Cruttwell was not a man of natural charm. Even his best friends
accepted that he was a misogynist, and his manners were not those which
might have been expected from a man of his aristocratic background.[88]
In general, his faults made him more tolerant of faults in others – in
other men, at least. Unfortunately, Waugh's chief shortcoming was
calculated to provoke maximum frustration in his tutor:[89] he cared
nothing whatever for the subject he was meant to be studying. They
clashed over Waugh's drunkenness and total lack of productivity, and
when Waugh left his viva with a poor third Cruttwell had little sympathy:

> I cannot say that your 3rd does you any thing but discredit: espe-
> cially as it was not even a good one; and it is always, at least, fool-
> ish to allow oneself to be given an inappropriate intellectual label.
> I am bound to tell you that your Scholarship will lapse next term. I
> hope that you will soon settle into some sphere where you will give
> your intellect a better chance than in the History School.[90]

Over the coming years, Cruttwell would badmouth his errant student
to his future mother-in-law[91] and – according to Waugh's grandson –
attempt to blackball him from various jobs.[92] In return, Waugh proved
as loyal in enmity as he did in friendship.

But Waugh also had reason to be grateful to Cruttwell, beyond a
mildly comic name and morbidly fascinating pipe-spit. For reasons best
known to himself, Cruttwell refrained from sending Waugh down before
he reached those disappointing final Schools.[93] Perhaps he hoped that,
against all evidence to the contrary, Waugh would realize his potential.
If so, he was right; but he would live to regret it.

The Oxford Canal

In Oxford, famous centre of book learning and studious graft, another life has always flowed alongside the quads and colleges. Before the advent of road haulage, Oxford's waters carried coal, paper and people from north to south and back again. And in this city, in the middle of England, the River Thames and the Oxford Canal meet not once but twice: by the railway station through the Sheepwash Channel, and to the north at Duke's Cut.[94] It must have been at Duke's Cut that, during Evelyn

Waugh's second undergraduate year, Harold Sissons first arrived in Oxford from the Thames. He might have moored near the old Trout Inn, where Waugh and his friends occasionally met to celebrate an invented vice called 'vanoxism'. (None of them really knew what 'vanoxism' was supposed to be; the term originated in a dream of Richard Pares', and John Sutro thought it had something to do with 'scourging raw beef with lilies'.[95]) Sissons was a 'strange figure', an early-twentieth-century escapee from the rat race who had taken to the water with his 'wife and unkempt family'. He was rich, he said, and proposed to refinance the defunct *Cherwell* magazine. For a time Waugh's friend Christopher Hollis went out to Sissons's barge at Godstow and worked as the magazine's editor, but 'with the autumn mists' the 'man of mystery' untied his boat and 'sailed away' again 'into whatever land of hallucination he naturally inhabited'.[96]

Consciously or otherwise, Sissons was following a path laid down for him by the Scholar Gypsy, a mythic figure who could, according to legend, still be glimpsed among the hills and woodlands that surrounded Oxford. Tales of the Gypsy date back more than three hundred years. They tell the story of an impoverished undergraduate who, tired of his money worries and life of study, runs away to share his learning with a band of travellers, and in return gains their wisdom.[97] Matthew Arnold retold the legend in 1853; in his poem the Gypsy, relieved of his worldly cares, becomes so attuned to the natural order that his life is indefinitely preserved with the turn of the seasons:

> And, above Godstow Bridge, when hay-time's here
> In June, and many a scythe in sunshine flames,
> Men who through those wide fields of breezy grass
> Where black-wing'd swallows haunt the glittering Thames,
> To bathe in the abandon'd lasher pass,

Have often pass'd thee near
Sitting upon the river bank o'ergrown;
Mark'd thine outlandish garb, thy figure spare,
Thy dark vague eyes, and soft abstracted air –
But, when they came from bathing, thou wast gone![98]

For those who, like the Scholar Gypsy, were jaded by university life, the rivers and canals beckoned. They could be followed to other worlds, to 'land[s] of hallucination' or simply of escape. In 'The Balance', the first short story Waugh wrote after leaving university, the protagonist (Adam) takes an overdose in a cheap Oxford hotel. When it fails he substitutes geographical for corporeal egress and walks out of the city along a towpath. He has paused on a bridge and is looking down at the water when a swan, flying low to the river, breaks up his reflection. Adam converses with the image as it re-forms. It is here, in this space between worlds, that he debates the fragility of existence with another self which, in its transience, foresees his inevitable death.

The existential anguish of 'The Balance' seem a departure from the superficial, cavalier way in which death is treated in Waugh's university fiction. In 'Edward of Unique Achievement', for example, a young killer disposes of his dagger in the canal at the end of George Street. It disappears with a splash, and his murderous act is just as neatly covered up. 'The Balance' concerns suicide rather than homicide, and enters into philosophical debate on the will to live. However, Adam's conclusion points to an ephemeral viewpoint which has much in common with the earlier stories. Adam's ferocious 'appetite for death' appears to vanish in the night, and Adam remarks that it may be 'appeased by sleep or change or the mere passing of time'.[99]

In the satires which follow 'The Balance', life and death are treated equally lightly. Few characters are in control of their own fates, but are pushed around by the demands of war,[100] the whims of malign and misled governments[101] or simply more effective personalities.[102] Death and catastrophe are often the result of a ridiculous accident or the highly unlikely alignment of disparate circumstances: a grazed foot,[103] an exploding toilet,[104] a chance encounter with a deranged individual.[105] Typically, Waugh's characters are not free, like Adam, to walk out of their lives. If they do leave them, it is more usually the result of forcible ejection.

Alice's Shop

Nestled at 83 St Aldate's, facing the Tom Quad of Christ Church, is a tiny, 650-year-old building with a pointed roof. It used to be a grocery shop, and in the late 1850s and 1860s the children of Henry Liddell, dean of Christ Church, used to buy their sweets there. The shop was run by an elderly lady with a tremulous voice who, so the story goes, passed the time by knitting.

The shop caught the imagination of Henry Liddell's colleague, the Reverend Charles Lutwidge Dodgson. And when Dodgson, better known to the world as Lewis Carroll, began writing stories for Liddell's little daughter Alice, 83 St Aldate's was immortalized. In *Through the Looking Glass and What Alice Found There* (1871), the grocery's elderly proprietor is transformed into a bespectacled, discourteous sheep, and her establishment is reborn as the Old Sheep Shop.[106]

Inside the Sheep Shop, nothing will stay still long enough to be looked at properly and the building – whose real-life counterpart was prone to flooding due to the proximity of the underground Twill mill stream – temporarily dissolves to leave Alice and the elderly sheep stranded in a boat in the middle of a river.[107]

By the time Waugh went up to Oxford, Alice and Lewis Carroll were famous and 83 St Aldate's was already known locally as 'Alice's Shop'.[108]

As a schoolboy, Waugh had been captivated by the whimsy, humour and menacing undertone of the *Alice* stories. During his Easter vacation of 1922 he read *Alice in Wonderland* again;[109] three years later, when he began his exile as a schoolmaster in North Wales, he packed the book in his bag.[110]

Waugh was rereading *Alice* at the most influential points of his life. His world, like the world down the rabbit hole, was suddenly brighter and more fantastical: a place of misrule where anything could happen, and frequently did. When Waugh came to write about Oxford in *Brideshead Revisited*, he did so in Carroll-like terms:

> I was in search of love in those days, and I went full of curiosity and the faint, unrecognized apprehension that here, at last, I should find that low door in the wall, which others, I knew, had found before me, which opened on an enclosed and enchanted garden…[111]

But it wasn't just the wonder of Carroll's creations that held a lasting fascination for Waugh. His plots also reflect their absurdity and confusion – and even their cruelty. Waugh's second novel *Vile Bodies*, written in his most acerbic phase, opens with two epigraphs from *Through the Looking Glass*. In the first, an exhausted Alice is told she must keep running just to stay in the same place. In the second, a contemptuous Tweedledum asks the crying Alice: 'I hope you don't suppose those are real tears'?[112]

Vile Bodies is a novel of acid comedy and whirling chaos, in which characters live life in a lane so fast that they crash (literally, in one case). It is also a narrative in which deep emotion is suppressed in the deceptively casual and carefree language of the roaring twenties. Here, for example, are Adam and Nina discussing their upcoming marriage:

> 'I don't know if it sounds absurd,' said Adam, 'but I do feel that a marriage ought to go on – for quite a long time, I mean. D'you feel that too, at all?'
> 'Yes, it's one of the things about a marriage!'
> 'I'm glad you feel that. I didn't quite know if you did. Otherwise it's all rather bogus, isn't it?'[113]

Waugh's first marriage imploded during the writing of *Vile Bodies*, and Adam and Nina never make it to the altar. Soon after the book's publication, Waugh vented his frustration with what he saw as a society wedded only to transience, in his *Daily Mail* article 'Let the Marriage Ceremony Mean Something': 'We see the marriages of our friends and relations going down like ninepins all round us,' Waugh wrote, 'and the idea of permanence becomes faint.'[114]

The bright world of wonderland might be fun, but it was not real. Emotion could never be sincere there, and its whole edifice might dissolve – like the Old Sheep Shop – at a moment's notice.

The Oxford Union

On Waugh's first trip to the Oxford Union he was impressed by the 'really good' speech of an Indian debater. [115] The man was in fact a Sri Lankan, S.W.R.D. Bandaranaike, who was reading Modern Greats at Christ Church. Like many Union men, Bandaranaike had his eye on a political career. He would eventually achieve his goal, though he might have wished he hadn't.

At Oxford, Bandaranaike's ambitions were stalled. He served as Union secretary in Michaelmas term 1923, while Waugh's friend Christopher

Hollis was president.[116] According to Hollis, at this point Bandaranaike was an imperialist. However, when he stood for the presidency, he encountered a depth of hostility that turned him against the Empire for good. In *The Oxford Union*, Hollis remembers how 'word had gone out among the old life-members ... that it would be undesirable that the Union should have a President who was not white'. These University alumni had turned out to vote in sufficient numbers to 'ensure his defeat'.[117] As well as this coordinated racism, Waugh's *A Little Learning* provides an insight into the casual prejudice Bandaranaike and his fellow non-white students encountered every day:

> Asiatics abounded, and these were usually referred to as 'black men' whether they were pale Egyptians or dusky Tamils. There was no rancour in the appellation; it was simply that these exotics seemed as absurd among the stones of Oxford as topeed tourists in the temples and mosques of the orient; there was no hint of deliberate personal contempt; still less of hostility. It struck us as whimsical to impute cannibalism to these earnest vegetarians. We may have caused offence.[118]

In 1932 Waugh published *Black Mischief*. It was and is a contentious book, but the source of its controversy has shifted over time. The narrative follows the fortunes of the emperor Seth as he attempts to modernize the fictional African kingdom of Azania. Seth was partially modelled on Ethiopia's Haile Selassie but, we are told, acquired his appetite for 'Progress' at Oxford. Seth was a contemporary of Waugh's infamous anti-hero Basil Seal, and Seal uses the pretext of their once having lunch together to insinuate himself into the Azanian political hierarchy. As Bandaranaike was the only 'oriental' whom Waugh met at university,[119] it is possible that the plot also draws on his circumstances and political ambitions.

In the 1930s it was *Black Mischief*'s supposedly obscene content that
caused offence and set Waugh, newly converted, at odds with the
Catholic press.[120] For a contemporary reader, the representation of Seth
and his people is more likely to pose problems. On his return to Azania,
Seth finds that his plans to transform the country do not translate and are
frequently misunderstood. The boots he issues to his barefoot army are
eaten, his state-of-the-art road must be built around a broken down car,
and – in the biggest misunderstanding of all – condoms are reinterpreted
as fertility charms. When the political wheel turns against Seth, he is
assassinated. The same fate awaited Bandaranaike, whose racial policies
and divisive Sinhala Only Act led to his shooting in 1959 by a Buddhist
monk.

At first glance, it looks as if *Black Mischief* simply rehearses the same
prejudices Waugh displayed at Oxford and remembered in *A Little
Learning*: modernity is as ridiculous in backwards Azania as turbans
among the 'stones of Oxford'. But there is another way of reading
the novel. In *Evelyn Waugh's Satire*, Naomi Milthorpe suggests that it is
modernity in general, not its misguided application to a non-modern
world, that Waugh attacks in *Black Mischief*. According to Milthorpe,
Seth's promotion of biological sterility is Waugh's comment on the
'sterility of the modern European age', which has emptied itself of
meaning and vitality because it has turned its back on the Catholic
Church, the original source of both.[121]

Milthorpe's idea is supported by Waugh's treatment of Seth, who,
for all his fads and growing instability, is not an absurd character. His
death is related with a staccato lyricism at odds with the novel's earlier
ironical tone, and Seal's determination to avenge him is motivated by
principle rather than his usual self-interest. He returns to London still
brooding over the catastrophe, leading his friend Sonia to remark: 'D'you

know, deep down in my heart I've got a tiny fear that Basil is going to turn serious on us...!'[122] Seth's tragedy is not the presumption that he, a black man, can aspire to the giddy heights of modernity preserved only for 'civilized' whites but rather the assumption that modernity is worth implementing in the first place.

St John's College
& Campion Hall

Four hundred and fifty years ago, Queen Elizabeth I visited St John's College, Oxford. She was greeted by Edmund Campion, a young and brilliant scholar so admired by his undergraduates that they copied his mannerisms and patterns of speech. Campion performed well during the royal visit, but he was already suffering from religious doubts. He was attracted to Catholicism, which had been the country's official religion until 1552, but if he recanted the newly re-established Protestant faith it would be the end of a promising career and possibly his life.

Four years after Elizabeth's visit to St John's, Campion surrendered to his conscience and fled first to Ireland and then, barefoot, to Rome. He became a Jesuit, was ordered back to England and in 1581 was convicted of treason against the queen he had once impressed with his oratorical wit. He was hung, drawn and quartered, and died affirming both his faith and his loyalty to Elizabeth.[123]

In 1934 Evelyn Waugh began a biography of Edmund Campion.[124] It wasn't the first book he'd written since his conversion, but it was the first to have an explicitly Catholic theme. He chose Campion, he said, largely to honour the priest who had instructed him in his new religion: Father Martin Cyril D'Arcy, the recently appointed master of Oxford's Campion Hall.[125] The hall was due to move to a new, grander building and Waugh privately arranged to help fund the enterprise with the book's profits.[126]

There were other motivations for *Edmund Campion* besides gratitude. Waugh hoped the biography would improve his standing in Catholic intellectual circles, where his reputation was constantly under attack from the editor of *The Tablet*.[127] More importantly, however, Waugh wanted the book to change not just how he was seen but also who he was. Campion would be his role model, and writing about his life an act and statement of faith. Campion had turned his back on high society to obey his conscience; Waugh too wanted to give up his occasionally glamorous yet rootless existence. Campion had joined the Jesuits. Waugh's plan was less dramatic, but equally transformative. He wanted to get married.

The object of Waugh's love was the teenage Laura Herbert. Like both Waugh and Campion, Laura had been brought up Protestant but converted to Catholicism. However, while Waugh's reception into the Church had isolated him further from his family (Arthur infamously referred to Evelyn's 'perversion to Rome'),[128] all the Herberts had converted together, shortly after the death of Laura's father. Laura was already part of a Catholic community to which Waugh desperately wanted to belong. Unfortunately, this draw was also a stumbling block. Laura's mother Mary was not thrilled about her romantic entanglement with a divorcee who was regularly denounced in the Catholic press. Moreover, he was thirty-one to Laura's eighteen. A book of impeccable Catholic values would, Waugh hoped, help to assuage the Herberts' misgivings,[129] but this concern was secondary to the grace which might be his through its writing.

Waugh thought he 'could reform' if Laura agreed to be his wife, but was convinced of the fundamental 'awfulness of my character'.[130] Writing about Campion allowed Waugh to meditate on a gentle role model, known for his emotional restraint. He found Campion's virtues almost impossible to emulate, but never doubted that his faith saved him from being a worse man than he believed himself to be. 'You have no idea how much nastier I would be if I was not a Catholic', he half-apologised to Nancy Mitford during one of their spats. 'Without supernatural aid I would hardly be a human being.'[131]

In 1936 Waugh's prayers were answered. *Campion* had been published the previous September; in the spring, Waugh learned that it had won the prestigious Hawthornden Prize, awarded to writers under forty-one for an imaginative literary work of particular brilliance. The Hawthornden was understood as a stamp of approval for all Waugh's works,[132] but he was delighted that it had been given to this particular book.[133] Hot on the heels of the award ceremony came news from the Vatican that his marriage to Evelyn Gardner[134] had been annulled. His Catholic credentials and single status were now assured, and he was free to marry – if Laura would have him. 'I can't advise you in my favour', he wrote to her, 'because I think it would be beastly for you, but think how nice it would be for me. I am restless & moody & misanthropic … In fact it's a lousy proposition.'[135]

Waugh might never attain Campion's humility, but he could be honest, and humble. This was good enough for Laura. Mr and Mrs Waugh might not have lived perfectly happily ever after, but Laura's love and the religion they shared protected Waugh from the grimmest aspects of himself.

Maltby's the Bookbinders

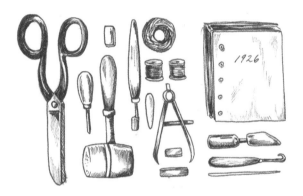

For 130 years Alfred Maltby & Sons bound Oxford's books, theses and manuscripts from their premises at 26–28 St Michael's Street.[136] They were Waugh's favourite binders, and from his student days to well into the 1940s he took his diaries there to be bound and his most precious books mended.[137]

Maltby's still use the techniques of the early 1700s to handcraft books from calf and goat skin, finishing them with gold tooling and marbled boards.[138] Waugh loved their tradition and attention to detail, but these soon proved expensive for an undergraduate of his means. Towards the end of his studies he ran out of money, and was forced to auction his fledgling collection.[139] Still, he stayed loyal to Maltby's and came back to them time and again in his wealthier years.

Since childhood, Waugh had been enchanted by lovingly produced books that were a joy to see, handle and smell as well as read. He'd enjoyed the free run of his father's well-appointed library, and his own juvenilia were printed onto handmade paper and leather-bound for posterity.[140] His delight in the physical object of the book was of a piece with his conviction that writing was itself not so much an art as a craft. He took satisfaction in seeing anything 'well done', from a boyhood watching 'deft' grocers patting butter into shape and drapers tearing fabric down neat lines to polishing his own rough drafts into well-turned phrases.[141] Even when his reviews were tepid, he could rely on appreciation for his 'memorably beautiful prose'.[142]

Language was Waugh's raw material, and he fashioned words into books as Maltby's fashioned leather and gold leaf into their covers. As such, words were not meant to have ideas of their own but required careful assembly in order to convey a writer's ideas accurately. In *A Little Learning*, Waugh offers this perspective as an article of faith:

> I believe that ... a boy [must] fully understand that a sentence
> is a logical construction and that words have basic inalienable
> meanings, departure from which is either conscious metaphor or
> inexcusable vulgarity.[143]

If readers failed to grasp the meaning of Waugh's words then this could only be because his material was insufficiently sculpted. To guard against this, he entered into long discussions concerning how his narratives should be read,wrote prefaces pointing to their central themes and,[144] where he could, revised published works to make his intentions clearer. His largest intervention was in the conclusion to *Unconditional Surrender*, which in the first edition sees Guy having two sons with his second wife, Domenica, as well as adopting the older Gervase, his widow Virginia's child by her lover.[145]

Waugh was frustrated that many of his readers thought this was meant to be a 'happy ending' instead of seeing, as he wrote to the academic and book collector John Sparrow, the irony that the 'true' Crouchback heirs stood to be disinherited and the family line corrupted by Guy's adopted son. Waugh proposed to sharpen the injustice in future editions of the book by making Guy's second wife childless.[146]

Waugh's Sword of Honour trilogy refines a theme he'd earlier explored during the decade following his conversion, in the black comedies *Black Mischief* and *Scoop!* In both novels words are debased from their 'inalienable meanings' and as a result become useless, like the new currency emperor Seth has printed but is universally rejected. Truth is everywhere displaced: John Courtney Boot is mistaken for William Boot, just as the false Crouchback would later usurp the authentic. Misunderstandings abound.[147]

Despite the farce of these pre-war novels, the power of such mis- and displacement to topple empires and ruin lives remains a constant threat. In *Officers and Gentlemen*, the second novel of *Sword of Honour*, this malevolent force breaks the surface. On the starving, constantly bombarded island of Crete, Guy Crouchback encounters some prisoners of war who have been abandoned to their fate by their captors. 'In a year or two of war', the narrator remarks, '"Liberation" would acquire a nasty meaning. This was Guy's first meeting with its modern use.'[148] Modernity is explicitly aligned with linguistic equivocality, and equivocality provides misdirection for shameful and immoral acts.

In these novels, when objective truth of language is elided, the result can be downright evil. Misused words were not only inelegant but also highly dangerous. For this reason, they must not be 'liberated' but marshalled, printed, stitched together and properly contained.

Pubs

For most of Oxford's history, undergraduates were banned from the city pubs. Things only changed in the twentieth century, on the return of World War II veterans to their disrupted studies. The University's authorities appreciated the absurdity of denying these men, young in years but heavy with experience, the freedom to drink wherever they pleased.[149]

Back in the 1920s Waugh and his friends had to be more resourceful. One stratagem was to get invited to a pub by a don or a Master's graduate, and some establishments stretched this definition to allow a regular 'host' to entertain a large number of brand-new friends on any given night of the week. The Chequers for example, which has stood since the sixteenth century at 131 High Street, housed a 'distressed and alcoholic clergyman' who was very happy to be bought drink after drink in return for insisting to the University proctors that all the students in the pub were there as his guests.[150]

After Waugh's friend Alastair Graham was sent down, things were different. The University curfew no longer applied to him and on his weekend visits the two boys would see 'little of the university, spending our … evenings in the Oxford inns frequented by townees'.[151] Graham is usually assumed to be the model for *Brideshead Revisited*'s Sebastian Flyte. There are plenty of reasons for thinking this, chief among them Waugh's occasional writing of 'Alastair' for 'Sebastian' in his manuscript for the novel.[152] And Evelyn and Alastair's tours of 'the Turf, the Nag's Head, the Druid's Head, the Chequers and many [other inns]'[153] are mirrored in those made by Charles and Sebastian.

If there was freedom in breaking University bounds, the same was true of drinking. As Waugh recalls in *A Little Learning*, there was defiance in the excessive behaviour in which he and his friends indulged. Prohibition had just come into force in the United States, and on 8 February 1922 the Oxford Union passed a motion in favour of extending the ban to England. In this climate, getting stinking drunk could be glorified as an assertion of autonomy.[154] In his first travel book, Waugh even went so far as to associate drinking with patriotism:

> Every true-born Briton lives under a fixed persecution mania that someone is always trying to prevent him from getting a drink. Of course, this is true, but the significant thing is how little they have succeeded. They have been at it now for nearly a hundred and fifty years, and it is still the easiest thing in the world to get drunk in England, and, if that is what is desired, to remain drunk for weeks at a time.[155]

All this might be very well but, as everyone knows, drinking ends with a hangover. The fun cannot go on forever. While many of Waugh's books celebrate the delights of drinking, they also chart its malice. In *Brideshead* it is Cara, Lord Marchmain's lover, who first pierces the bubble of Sebastian and Charles's wine-soaked happiness:

> 'Sebastian drinks too much.'
>   'I suppose we both do.'
>   'With you it does not matter. I have watched you together. With Sebastian it is different. He will be a drunkard if someone does not come to stop him. I have known so many. Alex [Lord Marchmain] was nearly a drunkard when he met me; it is in the blood. I see it in the way Sebastian drinks. It is not your way.'[156]

Cara is too late. Sebastian spirals into alcoholism, and it is at this point that he becomes more than a simple stand-in for Alastair Graham. While Sebastian's withdrawal from his family and friends does to some extent mirror Graham's eventual reclusivity, it was his successor in Waugh's affections, the young Olivia Plunket Greene, who was the true alcoholic. Evelyn fell in love with Olivia at a low ebb: a university and art-school failure, on the brink of taking an ignominious job as a schoolmaster.[157] Both Olivia and Evelyn drank too much, and Olivia did not stop. She became increasingly dependent on alcohol and continued to live with her mother until she died of breast cancer at the age of fifty-one.[158] After her death, Olivia's mother wrote to tell Waugh that

> You were so often in her thoughts. She told me how you gave her £5 – & she brought it here to use it on caviare – to eat when she was well – but she never got well – & the £5 is still here…[159]

Waugh describes Olivia in similar terms to Sebastian. While in *A Little Learning* Olivia is 'a little crazy', 'truth-loving and in the end holy',[160] in *Brideshead* Sebastian's sister Cordelia reflects:

'I've seen others like him, and I believe they are very near and dear to God. ... Everyone will know about his drinking; he'll disappear for two or three days every month or so, and they'll all nod and smile and say ... "Old Sebastian's on the spree again," and then he'll come back dishevelled and shamefaced and be more devout for a day or two in the chapel. ... Then one morning, after one of his drinking bouts, he'll be picked up at the gate dying, and show by a mere flicker of the eyelid that he is conscious when they give him the last sacraments. It's not such a bad way of getting through one's life.'[161]

A.L. Rowse, Waugh's contemporary at Oxford, had little time for this kind of piety. To him a drunk was a 'bloody fool', not a holy one, and he annotated his personal copies of *Brideshead Revisited* and *A Little Learning* accordingly. 'Silly nonsense', he writes where Lord Brideshead remarks that 'God prefers drunkards to a lot of respectable people.'[162] But Waugh, for such a merciless delineator of people's faults, frequently showed tenderness towards alcoholics. In *A Little Learning*, for example, Waugh describes his friend Alfred Duggan as 'always tight', but praises him for overcoming what he calls an 'inherited disability'.[163] Like Sebastian, Alfred's predicament is not the result of poor willpower but 'in the blood' and deserving of sympathy. In *Put Out More Flags* compassion is also extended to the elegant and impassive Angela Lyne, who collapses at a cinema in a drunken stupor. Basil Seal, usually the last person to consider another's feelings, steps in to rescue Angela's dignity as well as (in a limited way) her liver:

'... I think it's pretty mean of you to drink without me as you've been doing ... next time you want to go on a bat, let me know. Just ring me up and I'll come round. Then we can drink together.'
    'But I want to so often, Basil.'
    'Well, I'll come round often. Promise me.'
    'I promise.'

> ... in general the new arrangement worked well. Angela drank
> a good deal less and Basil a good deal more than they had done for
> the last few weeks and both were happier as a result.[164]

In a 1953 interview Waugh declared that, although willing to excuse almost any individual failing, he could most readily forgive dipsomania.[165] Perhaps this was because he shared the weakness. Even at Oxford, in very drunken company, he was often the most intoxicated person in the room and could frequently be found 'sitting in a high chair, his head lolling to one side, helplessly drunk'.[166] In the 1950s he cheerfully admitted to being 'absolutely mad ... off my onion'[167] as a result of bromide poisoning; but the poisoning was itself the result of mixing chloral and bromide (then prescribed as a sleeping draught) with 'reckless quantities of crème de menthe'.[168] Towards the end of his life he 'cut down' to seven bottles of wine and three bottles of spirits a week.[169]

Waugh first loved Alastair, then Olivia. Both of them drank too much, and so did he. Olivia drank herself to death, and Evelyn's drinking undoubtedly hastened his own demise. In their shared dependency, the character of Sebastian already refracts Alastair, Olivia and Evelyn – and there is a further connection between the four. Sebastian is a 'cradle Catholic' who, when drink takes hold, is given protection in a holy order. Alastair, Olivia and Waugh were all Catholic converts.

Thus far, the consanguinity between drunkenness and godliness seems a little murky,

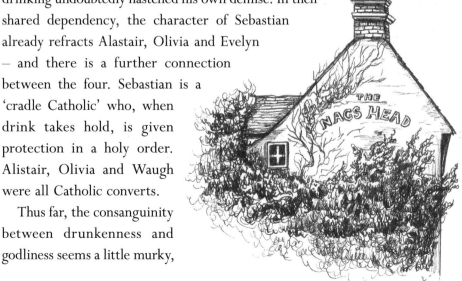

born of circumstance rather than theology. Did Waugh only think of alcoholics as 'holy' because he knew and loved some devout drunks? Surely not. He too was a drunk, but would never have described himself in such terms. Perversely, though, it may be within Waugh's awareness of his own inadequacies that a more substantial link between addiction and faith can be discovered. In his 1930 article 'Converted to Rome: Why It Has Happened to Me', Waugh characterized the difference between Protestant and Catholic mindsets as one of denial, versus acknowledgement, of sinfulness:

> The Protestant attitude seems often to be, 'I am good; therefore I go to church,' while the Catholic's is 'I am very far from good; therefore I go to church.'[170]

Few vices are as obvious as that of constant drunkenness, as Angela Lyne learned to her cost. For Waugh, the alcoholic was constantly confronting his or her own sinful nature, and therefore constantly aware of the imperfection which all fallen humanity shares, but generally does not admit. Such knowledge caused pain but, in his catechism, also a truthfulness that brought sinners closer to their God. As Cordelia remarked of Sebastian: 'No one is ever holy without suffering.'[171]

The Railway Station

On the evening of Wednesday, 28 November 1923, Evelyn Waugh boarded the Penzance–Aberdeen service from Oxford's Great Western Railway station[172] in a large company of students and a few college dons. They hired a private dining car, and got through most of their five-shilling menu – *Hors d'Œuvres*, *Crème de Celeri*, Fillet of Sole, Roast Chicken and *Mousse Framboise* – before reaching Leicester. There, they alighted and took the next train back to Oxford to finish off their cheese and salad.[173] Harold Acton made a speech, and thirteen of the group signed Waugh's menu.

This was the first meeting of the Railway Club, founded by Waugh's friend John Sutro. He was a sweet and gentle man, if a little ungainly. Waugh described him as 'singular and endearing',

> as though a whimsical taxidermist had secured some transitional anthropoid specimen, stripped it of its outer hide and replaced it with the skin of a rosy and robust baby, crowned the head with a soft brown wig and set it with large, innocent blue eyes...[174]

For many, Sutro's assembly was just one of Oxford's ingenious ways of getting around the ban on local pubs. As well as the Railway Club, Waugh also belonged to the White Rose Club, which drank to the 'Bavarian pretender' without really knowing who he was, and, despite his professed Conservatism, to the New Reform Club (founded by Lloyd George).[175] But the Railway Club, fuelled by Sutro's genuine enthusiasm for all things locomotive, was special. It carried on long after the friends had gone down. Its dinners became increasingly elaborate, its reputation grew and a rapidly expanding membership soon found itself greeted by small welcoming committees as it puffed through the Midlands countryside.[176]

When he was an elderly man, Waugh's thoughts turned back to the Railway Club. In autumn 1963, forty years since their first trip, he and Sutro decided to stage a reunion (pp. 23–4). They would meet at Paddington Station on 14 November, with as many original members as they could muster, and dine in the Pullman car of the *Brighton Belle*. Of those who signed Waugh's original five-shilling menu, Cyril Connolly, Harold Acton and Terence Greenidge accepted the invitation.[177] Peter Quennell and Waugh had long since fallen out. The older members, including 'Doggins' the sympathetic doctor and Tamil scholar Sydney

Roberts, were dead. So too was Richard Pares. Waugh had tried to coax Alastair Graham out of hiding in Wales for the occasion, but failed.[178]

Waugh did not enjoy the evening, which he described to another Oxford friend as 'an assembly of ghosts'.[179] It made him feel old. Sunk back in his seat, he could not hear most of the conversation and 'Harold Acton made a very long speech with his back to us'.[180] The whole thing resembled *Basil Seal Rides Again*, published earlier that year. In the book's opening scene, the eponymous Seal attends a prize-giving evening for his old friend Ambrose Silk (a fictionalized Harold Acton) and carries on a private conversation during an after-dinner address:

> 'There's a row now.'
>   'Some sort of speech.'
>   'And a lot of fellows saying: "Shush".'
>   'Exactly. I can't concentrate. What did you say?'[181]

Like the Railway Club dinner, Basil Seal was a shadow of his former glory. On his first outings in the 1930s and 1940s,[182] Waugh's anti-hero was dashing and amoral, modelled on his Oxford contemporaries Basil Murray and Peter Rodd. Now, he was an unflattering self-portrait: fat, florid and old before his time. By contrast Harold Acton and John Sutro had not changed at all. Towards the end of his life, Waugh became convinced that his deafness, rudeness and boring conversation rendered him – like Basil – unfit for company. Nevertheless, just as Seal stuck by Silk, Waugh stuck by Sutro. He might have lost his confidence, but he kept his loyalty. 'The general verdict', he wrote in his diary: 'Anyway John is enjoying it.'[183]

The Old Palace

The underground stream that
flows past the foundations
of Alice's Shop continues its
journey below the Old Palace,
or Bishop King's Palace, in Rose
Place.[184] The palace is formed of
two half-timbered houses, the
older of which dates back to the
sixteenth century.[185] This house
was bought in 1621 by a brewer
named Thomas Smith, who built
its neighbour and joined them
together to create one of the largest
houses in Oxford. The palace is named for
Robert King, Oxford's first bishop, and is now home
to Oxford's Catholic Chaplaincy.[186]

From 1926 to 1938 the Old Palace was home to Waugh's friend
Father Ronald Knox, the university chaplain.[187] Waugh first heard
Knox preach in 1924[188] and got to know him better while writing his
life of Edmund Campion.[189] The two priests were curiously similar, in

personality and reputation. Both were brilliantly promising scholars who made their names in Oxford through eloquent, charismatic and persuasive public speaking, and both were ordained in the Church of England before becoming Catholics. If the sacrifices involved were lighter for Knox, then they were still considerable; his father, an evangelical Anglican bishop, praised his son's intellectual achievements but disinherited him for his apostasy.[190]

Waugh and Knox grew closer during the Second World War, and the priest became one of Waugh's most valued friends. Knox, born in 1888, was fifteen years older than Waugh, but in some ways Waugh was more in tune with Knox's generation than his own. Waugh regarded the time Knox spent at Oxford as the University's golden period, and lamented how most of Knox's gifted fellow students had been wiped out by the First World War. Waugh's aversion to contemporary politics and society was echoed in Knox's favoured dismissal of the modern world as 'this revolting age'.[191] Few of his peers had any real sympathy with this view. More importantly, however, in Knox there coexisted the personal qualities Waugh prized most and could find nowhere else in the same man. He bridged a gap between Waugh's sharp-witted but non-Catholic friends, such as Nancy Mitford and Diana Cooper, and pious but slower companions whom he loved but found boring (and then felt guilty about it).[192] Knox was an accomplished writer, and turned his pen to a series of detective novels as well as Catholic apologetics and learned, stinging religious satires. It was a blessing for Waugh to know a fellow Catholic who could also make sophisticated literary critiques of his work.[193] Knox initially had misgivings about the worldlier aspects of *Brideshead Revisited* but was won over by Julia Flyte's impassioned monologue on sin. He loved *Helena* and was one of the most enthusiastic advocates of *Men at Arms*, the first novel in Waugh's *Sword of Honour* trilogy, which he compared favourably (good Greek scholar that he was) with the *Iliad*.[194] The appreciation was mutual. In 1949 Knox dedicated *Enthusiasm*, a 2,000-year history of religious asceticism, to Waugh. The dedicatee pronounced it 'the greatest work of literary art of the century'.[195]

In 1957 Knox was diagnosed with terminal cancer. He asked Waugh to act as his literary executor. Waugh agreed, and offered a further service to his dying friend: he would write his biography. *The Life of the Right Reverend Ronald Knox* was published in 1959. It had a launch of sorts at the Old Palace, which Waugh described to Daphne Acton, his and Knox's mutual friend,[196] as 'An absolutely ghastly vin d'honneur [*sic*] ... It was black with clergymen and I was deafened & asphyxiated.'[197]

Waugh had had little desire to write the book in the first place. It had involved heavy research, and Waugh knew he had no chance of being objective about his subject matter. Trying to imagine Knox's inner life also felt like impertinence, though Waugh had his blessing to try. He was motivated only by a wish to do his duty by Knox. For many years, the priest had wanted to write a sequel to *A Spiritual Aeneid*, which relates the circumstances of his conversion. He was now in no position to do this, and so Waugh did it for him.[198] The biography was itself a kind of sequel to *Campion*, a twinning born of the similarities between Waugh's subjects. The first was a meditation on a role model, and a statement of Waugh's good intent. The second was a labour of love.

Christ Church

Christ Church might not be Oxford's oldest college, but it is easily its grandest.[199] During the English Civil War Charles I used it as his royal retreat, first from the plague and then from the Roundheads. During the Civil War he ran his parliament from the Great Hall and his soldiers drilled in Tom Quad, the largest quadrangle in the city.

Christ Church's connections to the English Crown date back to its foundation in 1546. There had been a religious community on the site for as long as Oxford had existed: first, St Frideswide took sanctuary there in a company of noble virgins to avoid marriage to the local king, and practised healing miracles nearby at Binsey. Later, a male Augustinian community founded a monastery in her name. Then, in the sixteenth century, Cardinal Wolsey began to curb the power of England's monasteries and convents. He dissolved St Frideswide's and planned to replace it with Cardinal's College. After the cardinal's fall from grace, Henry VIII took over the endowment, denoted the old monastery church as Oxford's cathedral and renamed the foundation Christ Church.

Christ Church was the palatial residence of Waugh's friends Brian Howard and Harold Acton.[200] Brian Howard, whose bravado outstripped his wealth, nevertheless could afford the luxurious Canterbury Quad.[201] The historian A.L. Rowse was, like Acton, billeted in Meadow Buildings. While for Acton the splendid surroundings were very much par for the course, Rowse was bowled over:

> My rooms are beyond my wildest expectations ... Walking into the enormous sitting-room, I felt quite lost. Why, it is twice as big as our front room at home.[202]

In *Brideshead Revisited*, both Anthony Blanche and Sebastian Flyte are Christ Church men, and much of the action takes place in the college. The overwhelming majesty of its quads, cathedral and gardens are in perfect sympathy with Charles Ryder's wide-eyed delight in his new, glamorous friends. For such a rich source of aesthetic grandeur, however, Christ Church was not always kind to Aesthetes. College students who did not conform to conventional expectations of masculine behaviour were, if caught by the wrong group of 'hearties', in danger of being 'ducked in Mercury'.

The Mercury fountain, which sits in the middle of Tom Quad, has a long history of violation. It started life pragmatically enough, as a ready supply of water for extinguishing fires, but in 1817 its lead and bronze centrepiece was torn down by the high-spirited future prime minister, the fourteenth Earl of Derby. The pond's current incarnation of the Roman god was not put in place until 1928,[203] and so did not witness Anthony Blanche's own encounter with Mercury earlier in the decade.

In one of *Brideshead Revisited*'s most famous passages, Blanche ends up in the Tom Quad fountain. He recounts the episode to Charles Ryder with spirited defiance: 'You heard about [the students'] treatment of me on Thursday? It was too naughty. Luckily I was wearing my oldest pyjamas and it was an evening of oppressive heat, or I might have been seriously cross.' On being accosted by a group of twenty drunks wishing to throw him in the pond, Blanche declares that 'nothing could give me keener pleasure than to be manhandled by you meaty boys.' This provokes the desired embarrassment in these straitlaced heterosexuals, who then stand awkwardly by as Blanche gets into the fountain himself: 'it was really most refreshing, so I sported there a little and struck some attitudes, until they turned about and walked sulkily home.' Ryder knows that Blanche's actions and his witty recounting of them are a face-saving exercise, and that his repeated references to the ducking show that it remains 'much on his mind'. It was not, Ryder reminds us, the first time that 'Anthony had been ducked'.[204]

Blanche's attackers show a side of power that is neither beautiful nor cultured, enacted within a dazzling edifice that was, after all, founded on the ruins of an ancient religious community. Such knowledge lends an irony to *Brideshead*'s Christ Church setting; this profoundly Catholic novel owes much of its aesthetic pull to the pre-eminent monument of the power and wealth of Henry VIII's Church of England.

If so, then the irony is ultimately trumped by the narrative's confidence in a deeper history; in the chapel of the beleaguered Brideshead Castle, the tabernacle flame is relit and burns 'anew'. St Frideswide's legacy has not been effaced by Christ Church's glamour. She is the patron saint of both the city and the University. In the nineteenth century Edward Burne-Jones added her story to the College cathedral. She is depicted in stained glass, her pursuer King Algar struck blind by a lightning bolt.[205]

Oxford Botanic Garden

The Oxford University Botanic Garden is not a particularly quiet place. The Cherwell runs past it, and in summer the yells of capsizing punters can drown out the delicate patter of its Grade II-listed fountain. The garden walls cannot quite keep out the sound of traffic from Magdalen Bridge. But the Garden has its own kind of peace.

In *Brideshead Revisited*, Sebastian Flyte cannot believe that his friend Charles has never been to the Botanic Garden. 'I simply don't know where I should be without [it]', he confides, as they walk there together arm in arm. 'There's a beautiful arch there and more different kinds of ivy than I ever knew existed.'[206]

For someone like Evelyn Waugh, there was as much solace to be taken from the Garden's *kinds* of plants and its 'beautiful arch'[207] as in the flowers and trees themselves. He claimed to be not much interested in nature for its own sake, writing in *A Little Learning* that

> For most of my life I found greater joy in the works of man than of nature, until quite late, and now it is revulsion from the works of man that has constricted, rather than an approach to nature that has enlarged, me.[208]

In Waugh's novels, the natural world is usually only a force for good when properly contained. While Sebastian loves his Botanic Garden, in *Put Out More Flags* Barbara Sothill takes refuge from her cold wartime house, overrun with unruly refugees, in the warmth of her orangery. Both spaces are framed by human constructs: Sebastian's garden by walls and arches, the orangery by panes of glass. And when Sebastian speaks of the Botanic Garden's 'kinds' of ivy, he gestures to the fact that – in these few acres of garden at least – there is a place for everything, and everything is in its place.

Oxford, like most botanical gardens, organizes its specimens using a system that originates with the eighteenth-century botanist Carl Linnaeus (himself named for the Linden tree). In Linnaeus's time, natural scientists found themselves overwhelmed by the sheer variety of the specimens they were studying. Old plants might be known by several different names while new plants, with no names at all, were discovered daily. To make sense of this organic disarray, Linnaeus developed a method of scientific classification that organized matter into three 'kingdoms': animal, vegetable and mineral. Vegetables were then sorted into classes and subclasses, or orders, based on the number of stamens and pistils found within their flowers. There was even a category for flowerless plants. Any vegetable could be identified, labelled and sorted using Linnaeus's taxonomy and the system caught on quickly, especially in England.[209]

Linnaeus's approach to classification was itself informed by the concept of the Great Chain of Being, a theological idea that can be traced back to Plato and Aristotle. The chain is a hierarchy encompassing all naturally occurring objects, with God at the top and rocks and stones at the bottom. Plants sit just above minerals, and are themselves classed in importance from trees down to funghi. Humanity, being both animal and spiritual, has its place between angels and dumb beasts. The ordering of the chain is eternal and immutable.[210]

When Waugh converted to Catholicism in 1930, it was largely the Church's promise of an unbroken connection with the past that drew him.[211] Its unchanging Mass, eternal and immutable, is the subject of a short story he wrote soon after his conversion. In 'Out of Depth', a lapsed Catholic named Rip Van Winkle is transported by black magic into a London five hundred years in the future. The city has undergone some form of reverse colonization, and the original inhabitants eke out an existence on the banks of the Thames. Rip is adrift and frightened until the city's new overlords take him to Mass:

> Rip knew that out of strangeness there had come into being something familiar; a shape in chaos. Something was being done. Something was being done that Rip knew; something that twenty-five centuries had not altered; of his own childhood which survived the age of the world.[212]

The Botanic Garden was three hundred years old when Waugh went to Oxford; it is the oldest of its kind in England. In 1621, Henry Danvers, first Earl of Danby, leased 5 acres of land from Magdalen College in order to create a 'spacious illustrious physicke garden, completely beautifully walled and gated'. It was first provided for the benefit of the University's medical scholars, that they may be aided in their 'painfull happy satisfying Worke' through the study of 'all useful and delightful plants'.[213]

This busy, relatively small patch of nature possesses both qualities Waugh cherished in his adopted Church. The Botanic Garden might shelter thousands of medicinal plants, but for Waugh – and possibly Sebastian Flyte too – longevity and order were the true sources of its curative power.

Merton Street

Oxford scholars have been playing tennis in Merton Street since 1595, when the 'lusty and cheerful' sport was recommended as the best defence against the plague.[214] The Merton court is home not to lawn but to 'real' tennis, which is still played there according to rules established more than four hundred years ago.[215]

It was next door to this tennis court that Waugh planned to live, during autumn 1924, with Hugh Lygon. Waugh would have completed his Finals and be simply fulfilling the minimum period of residence required by the University in order for him to claim his degree. He would not even have to pretend to work any more, and could abandon himself to 'pure pleasure'.[216]

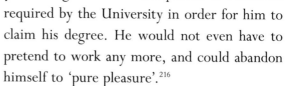

Hugh was a fey, dreamy boy, one of Oxford's 'aristocratic refugees from the examination system' harboured by Pembroke College.[217] Physically, he resembled Waugh's boyfriends Richard Pares and Alastair Graham,[218] and it is possible that Hugh and Evelyn were lovers too. A.L. Rowse certainly thought so, but he had a propensity to exaggerate any evidence of homosexual affairs and so his claim must be taken with a pinch of salt.[219] Hugh's sister Sibell agreed that Waugh was 'in love' with him,[220] but if true this does not necessarily mean that the feeling was mutual. Whatever the exact nature of Evelyn's relationship with Hugh, however, there is a good deal of him in *Brideshead Revisited*'s Sebastian Flyte. When Dorothy Lygon, another sister, read the book she told Waugh that Hugh gave her 'many pangs'.[221]

Waugh's dismal performance in his Finals scuppered the Merton Street plan, but his friendship with Hugh survived. He got to know Sibell and Dorothy ('Coote') as well as the other Lygon sisters Maimie and Lettice, and, following the break-up of his marriage to Evelyn Gardner, became a regular visitor to the family home at Madresfield Court. Much of *Black Mischief* was written in the Lygons' old nursery, which was set aside for his use.[222] The Lygons were Catholic; the chapel of Brideshead Castle is closely modelled on its Madresfield counterpart.[223]

In 1934 Hugh signed up for a small-scale expedition to the Arctic with the young explorer Sandy Glen. On a whim, Evelyn asked if he could come too. Glen agreed, and the three men set off on a trip that, according to Waugh at least, almost killed them. One day their trek took them to a small stream, easily fordable; they planned to cross it in relays, but within a matter of hours it had become treacherously swollen with flood water. Hugh got stuck in the middle; when Evelyn went to rescue him, he was knocked off balance by a fast-flowing lump of ice and the two men were swept away.[224] Waugh thought both of them were 'done for', but Hugh scrambled onto a glacier and Evelyn was able to crawl ashore.[225]

This near-death experience brought Evelyn and Hugh closer together. Sandy later remembered how Evelyn would spend the light Arctic nights confiding in Hugh about his father's obvious preference for Alec and his own love for Madresfield, where he always received a warm welcome.[226] Once perhaps lovers, Evelyn and Hugh had now become more like brothers.

Fate had a cruel irony in store for Hugh. Just two years after he narrowly escaped death by drowning, he tripped climbing out of a car and hit his head on the kerb. He cracked his skull, and never regained consciousness.[227]

Sebastian Flyte's self-imposed exile in Morocco has a ready biographical parallel in Alastair Graham's withdrawal from social life. However, his disappearance halfway through *Brideshead Revisited* is also suggestive of a more sudden loss. The Lygons, like the Flytes, struggled on in their brother's absence and Waugh stayed loyal to them all, even as their fortunes crumbled. In 1939 Waugh asked Maimie to be godmother to his eldest son,[228] and when in later life she struggled with alcoholism and disintegrating mental health he supported her. Waugh's friends had once lived in one of the country's most beautiful buildings. They had embraced Waugh and given him houseroom; before she died, Maimie Lygon was receiving cheques from him in the post.[229] Waugh may or may not have been in love with Hugh Lygon. He certainly loved the Lygons as a family he never had.

Notes

FOREWORD

1. See, e.g., EW to Laura Waugh, [c. 23 March] 1944, Evelyn Waugh Archive, Somerset.
2. EW, preface to the Uniform Edition of *Brideshead Revisited* (1959), Penguin Classics, London, 2011, pp. ix–x.
3. Arthur Waugh, 'Our Public Schools: XI. – Sherborne', *Country Life*, vol. 39, no. 1015, 17 June 1916, pp. 764–7; p. 766.
4. EW diary, 29 August 1943, Evelyn Waugh Collection 12.14–15, Harry Ransom Center (HRC), Austin TX.
5. Arthur Waugh, *One Man's Road*, Chapman & Hall, London, 1931, p. 371.
6. EW, Uniform Edition of *Brideshead Revisited*, p. 25.
7. Oxford Preservation Trust, matinée souvenir programme for the New Theatre, Oxford, 28 February 1930, p. 15.
8. EW, 'Was Oxford Worth While?', *Daily Mail*, 21 June 1930, p. 10.
9. EW to Dudley Carew, [May?] 1924, cited in Mark Amory (ed.), *The Letters of Evelyn Waugh*, Weidenfeld & Nicolson, London, 1980, p. 13.
10. EW, Uniform Edition of *Brideshead Revisited*, p. 53.
11. Dudley Carew diary, 15 December 1921, Nicholas Shakespeare Collection, Oxford.

EVELYN WAUGH'S CITY

1. Alexander Waugh, *Fathers and Sons*, Broadway, New York, 2007, p. 48.
2. EW, *A Little Learning*, Chapman & Hall, London, 1964, pp. 27, 34. The account Waugh gives here of an entire corps of Italian officers waiting to welcome an English lady writer with bouquets and freshly shaven faces is probably exaggerated; in *Waugh in Abyssinia* (Longmans, London, 1936), published a few years after the incident, Waugh only speaks of one officer, Captain Franchi, who flits 'between airport and railway station ... in a high state of amorous excitement' prior to his guest's arrival, but overcomes his disappointment gracefully (p. 246).
3. See, for example, the postscript to a letter from Alec Waugh to Arthur and Catherine Waugh, 6 December 1908, from Fernden School; Alec Waugh Collection, HRC.
4. Alec Waugh, *My Brother Evelyn and Other Profiles*, Cassell, London, 1967, p. 164.

5. EW, *A Little Learning*, p. 92; Matthew 5:13 reads: 'Ye are the salt of the earth: but if the salt have lost his savour, wherewith shall it be salted? It is thenceforth good for nothing, but to be cast out, and to be trodden under foot of men.'

6. Alec Waugh, *The Early Years of Alec Waugh,* Cassell, London, 1962, p. 21.

7. EW, 'Father and Son', *Sunday Telegraph*, 2 December 1962, pp. 4–5; p. 4.

8. Programmes for *Feed the Brute*, *The Man From Downing St* and *Beauty and the Beast* (performed January 1912) are available at Leeds University Library in the Fay and Geoffrey Elliot Collection.

9. 'I was much impressed by Newman's *Dream of Gerontius*, ... and in emulation composed a deplorable poem in the metre of Hiawatha, named *The World to Come*, describing the experiences of the soul immediately after death. The manuscript was shown to a friend of my father's who ... conceived the kindly idea of producing some copies on hand-made paper and binding them for my father's birthday. They were distributed within the family' (EW, *A Little Learning*, pp. 93–4). *The Pistol Troop Magazine*, produced by the Waugh and Fleming children, was also leather-bound and decorated with gold tooling. Max Fleming's copy is in the Fay and Geoffrey Elliot Collection, Leeds University Library; EW's is at the Evelyn Waugh Collection 8.5, HRC.

10. EW, *A Little Learning*, pp. 71, 95–6.

11. Alexander Waugh, *Fathers and Sons*, pp. 226–8.

12. EW, *A Little Learning*, p. 101.

13. The first two volumes of Mackenzie's *Bildungsroman* were published by Martin Secker, London, 1913–14.

14. EW, *A Little Learning*, p. 77.

15. EW Diary, 13 June [1921], Evelyn Waugh Collection 3.9, HRC.

16. EW, *A Little Learning*, pp. 96–100.

17. Alec Waugh, *The Loom of Youth*, Richard's Press, London, 1917, p. 244.

18. Alec's former housemaster, for example, scolded the young author thus: 'You cannot justify the thing: you will one day bitterly repent of writing it, if you have not already done so.' A.H. Trelawny Ross to Alec Waugh, 2 January 1918, from Devonport; Alec Waugh Collection, HRC.

19. EW Diary, 23 November [1921], Evelyn Waugh Collection 3.9, HRC.

20. EW, *A Little Learning*, pp. 102, 128.

21. Ibid.; EW Diary, 16 October [1921].

22. EW, 'The Youngest Generation', *Lancing College Magazine*, December 1921, p. 85.

23. EW Diary, 10 December [1921].

24. EW Diary, 15 [December 1921].

25. 'I can't get really interested in History. ... I don't want an academic career. I don't even know that I want Oxford awfully.' EW Diary, 11 November 1921.

26. EW, *A Little Learning*, p. 138.

27. Ibid., pp. 165–6, 176–7, 172.

28. Ibid., p. 171.

29. Martin Stannard, *Evelyn Waugh: The Early Years, 1903–1939*, J.M. Dent, London, 1986, p. 68; Selina Hastings, *Evelyn Waugh: A Biography*, Minerva, London, 1995, p. 98.

30. Peter Quennell, 'A Kingdom of Cokayne', in David Pryce-Jones (ed.), *Evelyn Waugh and His World*, Weidenfeld & Nicolson, London, 1973, pp. 23–38; p. 33.

31. Ibid., p. 38. Although Waugh and Quennell were friends at university, their relationship

became increasingly fraught: 'once we had both left Oxford, we ceased gradually to meet on amicable terms; and at length I joined the ranks of favourite bugbears ... who excited now his taste for ludicrous imagery, now his remarkable talent for invective' (ibid., p. 24).

32. Claud Cockburn, *In a Time of Trouble: An Autobiography*, Rupert Hart-Davis, London, 1956, p. 64.

33. A.L. Rowse's personal copy of *A Little Learning*, Fay and Geoffrey Elliot Collection, p. 181, Leeds University Library.

34. EW, *A Little Learning*, p. 191.

35. 'It was a male community. Undergraduettes lived in purdah.' EW, *A Little Learning*, p. 168.

36. In one effort, written to Waugh some time in 1923, Pares playfully dissects Waugh's last letter paragraph by paragraph, suggests footnotes to it and, here, draws attention to their relationship's subversion of normative gender roles by casting homosexual fantasy as romantic melodrama: 'I should stride up to Hampstead heath and in through the French window of your drawing room and – well, you know what happens when the hero (or heroine) strides in through the French Window of the drawing-room and finds the heroine (or is it hero?) sitting on the sofa ...'. Richard Pares to EW, [?1923], from Westfield, Surbiton; British Library, London, Add MS 81068.

37. Francis Fortescue ('Sligger') Urquhart (1868–1934), a Catholic, was dean of Balliol 1918–34.

38. See 'Balliol College', pp. 96–9.

39. When Evelyn Gardner became critically ill on what was supposed to be the Waughs' honeymoon cruise, EW met up with Alastair Graham and the pair toured Cairo brothels. In EW's account of the cruise (*Labels: A Mediterranean Journal*, Duckworth, London, 1930, pp. 90–94), he disguises Graham as a solicitor called Dennis and also invents the character of Geoffrey, so three men rather than the more intimate two enjoy Cairo's red-light district together. Gardner later asked Michael Davie, the editor of EW's diaries, 'I don't think he would have done that if he really loved me, would he?' Evelyn Nightingale (née Gardner) interview with Michael Davie, 24 February 1973, cited in Philip Eade, *Evelyn Waugh: A Life Revisited*, Orion, London, 2016, p. 132.

40. Hastings, *Evelyn Waugh*, pp. 106–10.

41. In 1962 Waugh told his friend Daphne Fielding: 'Alastair ... has become a recluse in Wales. I haven't seen him for 25 years. My closest chum once.' EW to Daphne Fielding, 30 July 1962, from Combe Florey; cited in Amory (ed.), *The Letters of Evelyn Waugh*, p. 589.

42. Hastings, *Evelyn Waugh*, p. 110.

43. EW, *A Little Learning*, pp. 207–8.

44. Ibid., pp. 209–15.

45. Many of EW's diary entries from this period are already partially fictionalized and narrated with *Decline and Fall*'s arch humour: 'Headmaster Banks wanders into the common-room in a blank kind of way and says "Oh I say, there are some boys in that end classroom. I don't know who they are. They may be a Set B in History or perhaps the Fourth Form, or are they the Dancing Class. Anyway, they've got their Latin books and they shouldn't have those so I think it would be best if someone took them in English."' EW Diary, 23 January 1925, Evelyn Waugh Collection 12.1, HRC.

46. EW Diary, 6 November 1925, Evelyn Waugh Collection 12.2, HRC.

47. Stannard, *Evelyn Waugh: The Early Years*, pp. 134–5.

48. EW, *A Little Learning*, p. 79.

49. According to EW's love rival Harman Grisewood (1906–1997), when Olivia definitively rejected EW, he burned her wrist with a cigarette (Harman Grisewood to Christopher Sykes, 2 April 1973; Christopher Sykes Collection 5.30, Georgetown University Library, Washington DC).

50. EW Diary, Evelyn Waugh Collection 12.3–4, HRC.

51. EW Diary, 12 December 1927, Evelyn Waugh Collection 12.4, HRC.

52. EW, 'Father and Son', p. 5.

53. EW to Harold Acton, [*c.* 7 August 1929], from Barford House, Warwickshire; cited in Amory (ed.), *The Letters of Evelyn Waugh*, p. 38.

54. EW, 'Preface', Uniform Edition of *Vile Bodies*, Chapman & Hall, London, 1965, p. 7.

55. Alexander Waugh, *Fathers and Sons*, p. 217.

56. EW Diary, 20 January 1925.

57. See, e.g., EW to Teresa Jungman, 14 November 1931, from Easton Court, Chagford; Evelyn Waugh Archive, Somerset.

58. Dalya Alberge, 'Lost Evelyn Waugh Letters Reveal Thwarted Love for "Bright Young Thing"', *Observer*, 21 July 2013, www.theguardian.com/books/2013/jul/21/evelyn-waugh-love-letters (accessed September 2016).

59. EW, *Ninety-Two Days*, Duckworth, London, 1934, p. 21.

60. Hastings, *Evelyn Waugh*, pp. 359, 364.

61. See, e.g., EW's condolences on his wife's third pregnancy: 'It is sad news for you that you are having another baby and I am sad at your sorrow. For myself, surrounded with the spectacle of a world organized to kill, I cannot help feeling some consolation in the knowledge that new life is being given ... I know your patience & resignation will be needed to the full in the coming year, and I thank god that you have them.' EW to Laura Waugh, [?March] 1940, from Gibraltar; cited in Amory (ed.), *The Letters of Evelyn Waugh*, p. 139. Amory dates the letter as April but it is more likely to be March.

62. Arthur Waugh to Kenneth McCaster, 25 August 1940; cited in Hastings, *Evelyn Waugh*, p. 408.

63. Martin Stannard, *Evelyn Waugh: No Abiding City 1939–1966*, J.M. Dent, London, 1992, pp. 40–41.

64. Waugh's first, chief detractor was Christopher Sykes, whose damning account of Layforce's actions on the island informed Anthony Beevor's *Crete* (Christopher Sykes, *Evelyn Waugh: A Biography*, HarperCollins, London, 1975; Anthony Beevor, *Crete: The Battle and the Resistance*, John Murray, London, 1991). Sykes's and Beevor's is the orthodox view, but this has been questioned in recent years. See, e.g., Donat Gallagher and Carlos Villar Flor, *In the Picture: The Facts behind the Fiction in Evelyn Waugh's 'Sword of Honour'*, Rodopi, Amsterdam and New York, 2014; and Eade, *A Life Revisited*.

65. EW Diary, 9 June 1943, Evelyn Waugh Collection 12.14–15, HRC.

66. Alexander Waugh, *Fathers and Sons*, p. 265.

67. Hastings, *Evelyn Waugh*, pp. 449–53.

68. EW Diary, 30 December 1943.

69. See, e.g., EW to Laura Waugh, [*c.* 23 March] 1944.

70. EW to Laura Waugh, [*c.* 10 June 1944], Evelyn Waugh Archive, Somerset.

71. There is a notable shift in Waugh's depiction of Jewishness following his experiences in Yugoslavia. These first found expression in the short story 'Compassion' (*Month* NS 2,

August 1949, pp. 79–98), which was later absorbed almost verbatim into *Unconditional Surrender* (Chapman & Hall, London, 1961). In 'Compassion', Major Gordon is distraught not to have been able to help Yugoslavia's Jewish refugees in any significant way, and many of his well-meant interventions have backfired. An army chaplain suggests that Gordon's attempt, while it did not benefit those he was trying to save, might nevertheless have done him good. The inference is that Gordon has grown in humanity.

72. EW Diary, 10 September 1945, Evelyn Waugh Collection 12.16–13.1, HRC.

73. EW, *Brideshead Revisited*, Chapman & Hall, London, 1945, front matter. Subsequent references are to this edition unless otherwise stated.

74. *Brideshead Revisited*, it is important to note, is not the first of Waugh's works to mourn a lost world or engage with the concept of regret. *Work Suspended* (note 50), for example, is also narrated in a wistful, if more clinical, tone and also makes use of the first person.

75. The True Cross is the name given to the actual, physical crucifix upon which Christ was killed.

76. In 1945, *The Tablet* published an early version of the first three chapters of *Helena*, making a composition period of at least five years. 'St. Helena Meets Constantius: A Legend Retold', *The Tablet*, vol. 186, no. 5511, 22 December 1945, pp. 7–10.

77. Stannard, *Evelyn Waugh: No Abiding City*, pp. 188–9, 239, 190–91.

78. Hastings, *Evelyn Waugh*, pp. 569, 499–500.

79. Just before the 1964 general election, for example, Waugh went on holiday to Spain in order 'to escape democracy' (EW postcard to Christopher Sykes, [*c.* 21 September] 1964, from Combe Florey; Christopher Sykes Collection 13.14, Georgetown University Library, Washington DC).

80. EW, *Frankly Speaking*, BBC Home Service, first broadcast 10.05–10.35 p.m., 16 November 1953, interview with Stephen Black, Jack Davies and Charles Wilmot.

81. In the *Spectator*, for example, R.D. Charques called it 'a lightly devotional, decorative, frequently entertaining, but not very substantial work of fiction' (vol. 184, no. 6381, 13 October 1950, p. 12).

82. Alexander Waugh, *Fathers and Sons*, p. 299.

83. See, for example, his exhortations to daughter Meg: 'I wish you could learn to rest. I don't mean by hoggishly sprawling about, but in setting about necessary tasks like sewing and writing letters in a leisurely way. That is real rest.' EW to Margaret Waugh, October 1962, private collection.

84. EW to Ann Fleming, 7 August 1963, cited in Amory (ed.), *The Letters of Evelyn Waugh*, p. 611. As Hastings notes, for Waugh boredom created the conditions required for depression. He used the two terms almost interchangeably: 'Evelyn suffered what he described in his diary as "degrading boredom", when, with nothing to distract him, he was overwhelmed with loneliness and depression' (*Evelyn Waugh*, p. 277).

85. Waugh wrote copious letters and articles regretting the recommendations of Vatican II during the early–mid-1960s; see 'The Botanic Garden', pp. 136–9.

86. EW, *A Little Learning*, p. 1.

87. See also 'The Railway Station', pp. 127–9.

88. EW, *A Little Learning*, p. 140.

89. This is made clear in various letters between Waugh and his agents and publishers, and the jacket of the American edition of *A Little Learning* refers to Waugh's 'three-volume autobiography.' EW, *A Little Learning*, Little, Brown, Boston MA and Toronto, 1964, cover copy.

90. This fragment is reproduced in full as an appendix to Barbara Cooke and John Howard Wilson (eds), *A Little Learning*, Oxford University Press, Oxford, 2017. Part of it is printed as an appendix to Alec Waugh's *Best Wine Last*, W.H. Allen, London, 1978.

91. EW, *A Little Learning*, p. 172.

92. A.L. Rowse, *A Cornishman at Oxford*, Jonathan Cape, London, 1965, p. 23. Confusingly, in his 'Isis Idol' article on Acton (see note 94) Waugh declared his friend contemptuous of aesthetes. However, from the context it is clear that Waugh uses the term historically, to mean the Aesthetes associated with the 1890s and the cult of Oscar Wilde.

93. EW, *A Little Learning*, p. 197.

94. EW [unsigned], 'Isis Idol No. 594; Mr Harold Acton (Christ Church), Editor of *The Oxford Broom*, Author of *Aquarium* etc.', *Isis*, 20 February 1924, p. 17.

95. EW, *Brideshead Revisited*, pp. 30–31.

96. Annotations to A.L. Rowse's personal copy of *A Little Learning*, pp. 229, 211, 166.

97. These figures are based on the entries found in Robert Murray Davis et al.'s *A Bibliography of Evelyn Waugh*, 2nd edn, Whitston, New York, 1986, updated to exclude pieces with the least reliable attribution and include more recent finds.

98. As well as his design for Richard Pares (see p. 9), Waugh made bookplates for his friend Roger Fulford and his lover Alastair Graham (fig. 21; Leicester, private collection).

99. See, e.g., C.C. and E.M. Molt, *Clent's Way*, Chapman & Hall, London, 1923; and Geraldine Waife, *Colleagues*, Chapman & Hall, London, 1923.

100. *Isis*, 21 February 1923, p. 7.

101. Personal conversations with Donat Gallagher, September–October 2016.

102. EW to Aitken, 29 January 1964; Evelyn Waugh Papers 7.230, Huntington Library, Pasadena CA.

103. EW Diary, [c. 10 September 1911], Evelyn Waugh Collection 3.2, HRC.

104. EW Diary, 10 June 1912.

105. See EW Diaries, 1914–21, Evelyn Waugh Collection 3.6–10, HRC.

106. EW Diary, 15 March [1921], Evelyn Waugh Collection 3.10, HRC.

107. Hodder & Stoughton, London, New York and Toronto, 1912.

108. *Edmund Dulac's Fairy-Book: Fairy Tales of the Allied Nations,* Hodder & Stoughton, London, 1916.

109. Arthur Waugh, 'On Reticence in Literature', in Elkin Mathews and John Lane (eds), *The Yellow Book: An Illustrated Quarterly* 1, April 1894, pp. 201–19.

110. Frances Fowle, 'Cover Design for the "Yellow Book"', 2000, www.tate.org.uk/art/artworks/beardsley-cover-design-for-the-yellow-book-n04171/text-summary (accessed 1 October 2016).

111. EW, *A Little Learning*, pp.145–6.

112. 'The Seven Deadly Sins. No III. The Wanton Way of Those that Corrupt the Very Young', *Cherwell*, 3 November 1923, p. 32. The poem is signed 'M.C.H.' *Cherwell* had a regular contributor signing him- or herself 'Socrates', and so the poem may be an in-joke.

113. 'Bertram, Ludovic and Ann', graphic art with open letter, *Isis*, 24 May 1923, p. 23.

114. Matthew Shaw, 'Children's Animal Tales', British Library, www.bl.uk/animal-tales/articles/childrens-animal-tales (accessed 4 October 2016).

115. EW, 'Isis Idol No. 594; Mr Harold Acton', p. 17.

116. *Cherwell*, 2 February 1924, p. 40.

117. EW, *A Little Learning*, p. 189.

118. EW, 'Youth', *London Mercury* 8, October 1923, p. 635, wood engraving of a young man with one foot in the cradle and one in the grave.

119. EW contributed five woodcuts to Bax's short-lived art and literature quarterly overall, and three to vol. 2, no. 6 (Chapman & Hall, London, January 1924): a man and woman in period dress on a half-canopied bed (p. 26), a satyr seated (p. 39) and two men (p. 43).

120. Personal conversations with Donat Gallagher, September–October 2016.

121. EW Diary, 10 December [1921].

122. Waugh claimed not to have put too much effort into his Union career, but Martin Stannard questions this on the grounds that Waugh was an ambitious debater at Lancing and stood for election as president of the Union in June 1923. *Evelyn Waugh: The Early Years*, pp. 75–6.

123. Personal conversations with Donat Gallagher, September–October 2016.

124. Gardiner ran a sustained campaign in the *Isis* against the double standards suffered by Oxford's first women undergraduates, and the future *Sunday Times* film critic Dilys Powell contributed a regular column to this effect ('What Every Woman Thinks'). Gardiner told Waugh that Powell wrote the article that sent him down – probably the 4 June 1924 column (p. 13), which blasts restrictions such as the prohibition of spontaneous conversations between one man and one woman extending beyond 'a few minutes' chat'. Gardiner to EW, 3 August 1963, from 12 King's Bench Walk; British Library, Add MS 81057.

125. EW, 'Seen in the Dark: The Oxford Super Cinema', *Isis*, 30 January 1924, p. 6.

126. Ibid., p. 5.

127. Virginia Woolf, 'The Cinema', 1926, Woolf Online, www.woolfonline.com/timepasses/?q=essays/cinema/full (accessed 6 October 2016).

128. EW, 'My Favourite Film Star', *Daily Mail*, 24 May 1930, p. 10.

129. *Isis*, 30 May 1923, p. xxii.

130. *Oxford Broom*, vol. 1, no. 3, June 1923, pp. 14–20.

131. *Cherwell*, 1 August 1923, pp. 14, 16–18.

132. See also 'Oxford: City of Memory', p. 54.

133. Robert M. McBride, New York, 1919; EW, *A Little Learning*, p. 189.

134. Hastings, *Evelyn Waugh*, p. 102; Stannard, *Evelyn Waugh: The Early Years*, p. 82.

135. EW, *A Little Learning*, p. 181.

136. Stannard, *Evelyn Waugh: The Early Years*, p. 84.

137. Hastings, *Evelyn Waugh*, p. 101.

138. EW, 'Wittenberg and Oxford', *Isis*, 14 February 1924, pp. 1–2.

139. *Cherwell*, 1 August 1923 and thereafter until 1929.

140. Davis et al., *A Bibliography of Evelyn Waugh*, p. 40.

141. For a detailed discussion of the way in which Waugh 'ruthlessly expunges interiority' from the characters of his early satirical novels, see Naomi Milthorpe, 'Real Tears: *Vile Bodies* and *The Apes of God*', in *Evelyn Waugh's Satire: Texts and Contexts*, Farleigh Dickinson University Press, Lanham MD and London, 2016, pp. 35–53.

142. EW, *A Little Learning*, p. 196.

143. Paul T. Heyne, 'To Thine Own Self Be True', *Cresset* 28, January 1965, pp. 24–5; p. 24.

144. EW, *Brideshead Revisited*, p. 20.

145. Quennell, 'A Kingdom of Cokayne', p. 23.

146. Edmund Wilson, for example, suggested that 'what has caused Mr Waugh's hero to plump on his knees is not, perhaps, the sign of the cross but the prestige, in the person of Lord Marchmain, of one of the oldest families in England.' 'Splendors and Miseries of Evelyn

Waugh', *New Yorker* 21, 5 January 1946, pp. 71–4, cited in Martin Stannard (ed.), *Evelyn Waugh: The Critical Heritage*, Routledge & Kegan Paul, London, 1984, pp. 245–8; p. 246.
147. EW, *Brideshead Revisited*, p. 90.
148. Ibid., p. 304.
149. EW, preface to the Uniform Edition of *Brideshead Revisited*, p. ix.
150. EW, *Brideshead Revisited*, p. 119.
151. EW, preface to the Uniform Edition of *Brideshead Revisited,* p. ix.
152. See, for example, Douglas Lane Patey's summary of the novel as forming a series of steps in Charles's loves 'from Sebastian through Julia to God'. *The Life of Evelyn Waugh*, Blackwell, Oxford and Cambridge MA, 2001, p. 226.
153. Hastings, *Evelyn Waugh*, p. 83.
154. EW, *Brideshead Revisited*, p. 27.
155. 'I can't explain why but [Charles] seemed to me a tiny bit dim…'. Nancy Mitford to EW, 22 December 1944, British Library, Add MS 81064.
156. Paula Byrne, *Mad World: Evelyn Waugh and the Secrets of Brideshead*, Harper Press, London, 2009, p. 46.
157. EW to Desmond MacCarthy, 27 July 1945; copy in Evelyn Waugh Archive, Somerset.
158. Derek Granger in interview for the 2011 DVD release of *Brideshead Revisited*, directed by Charles Sturridge and Michael Lindsay-Hogg, Acorn Media (Granada 1981).
159. Sybille Bedford, for example, commented that while the Oxford of *A Little Learning* is 'fascinating enough … the fun, the magic, are elsewhere'. 'The Loved and Loving One', *New York Herald Tribune Book Week* 15, November 1964, pp. 3, 25; p. 25.
160. John MacDougall to EW, 25 February 1963, British Library, Add MS 81062.
161. EW, *A Little Learning*, p. 193.
162. William Plomer, review of *A Little Learning* in *The Listener*, 10 September 1964, p. 397.
163. Anthony Burgess, 'Waugh Begins', *Encounter*, December 1964, pp. 64, 66, 68; reprinted in Stannard (ed.), *Evelyn Waugh: The Critical Heritage*, pp. 470–75; p. 474.
164. Waugh's brother Alec, however, loyally predicted that 'Never a Palinode' would be admired in parallel with the Oxford section of *Brideshead Revisited*. Review of *A Little Learning*, *Cosmopolitan* (US edn), November 1964, pp. 26–7.
165. Paul A. Doyle, review of *A Little Learning* in *Best Sellers* 24, 15 November 1964, p. 322.
166. See 'Pubs', p. 122.
167. See note 41.
168. See 'The Hypocrites Club', p. 93.
169. EW to Randolph Churchill, 18 September 1964, from Combe Florey; copy in Evelyn Waugh Archive, Somerset.
170. Charles Petrie, 'An Author's Yesterday', *Illustrated London News* 245, 3 October 1964, p. 503.
171. *A Little Learning* loose manuscript pages, Evelyn Waugh Collection 5.4 and 6.1–3, HRC.
172. Sutro to EW, 3 August 1963, from 26 Belgrave Square, London SW1; British Library, Add MS 81070.
173. EW to Sutro, 6 August 1963; Bodleian Library, Oxford, MS. Eng. c. 7256, fols 83–115.
174. EW to Diana Cooper, 6 June [1957], from Combe Florey; cited in Artemis Cooper (ed.), *Mr Wu and Mrs Stitch: The Letters of Evelyn Waugh and Diana Cooper*, Hodder & Stoughton, London, 1991, p. 240.
175. EW, *The Ordeal of Gilbert Pinfold*, Chapman & Hall, London, 1957, pp. 20–21.
176. Hastings, *Evelyn Waugh*, p. 562.

177. EW, *Brideshead Revisited*. p. 27.

178. EW, *A Little Learning*, p. 33.

179. John Gross, 'Waugh Revisited', *New York Review of Books* 3, 13 December 1964, pp. 4–5; p. 4.

180. EW, *A Little Learning*, p. 24.

181. Plomer, review of *A Little Learning*, p. 397.

182. V.S. Pritchett, 'Mr. Waugh's Exile', *New Statesman* 68, 25 September 1964, pp. 445–6; reprinted in Stannard (ed.), *Evelyn Waugh: The Critical Heritage*, pp. 459–64; p. 461.

183. EW, *Brideshead Revisited*, p. 197.

184. 'The Same Again Please', *Spectator*, 23 November 1962, pp. 11–14; p. 13.

185. Ibid.

186. Edward Yarnold, 'D'Arcy, Martin Cyril (1888–1976)', *Oxford Dictionary of National Biography*, Oxford University Press, Oxford, 2004; online edn, January 2011, www.oxforddnb.com/view/article/30998 (accessed 18 October 2016).

187. EW, *A Little Learning*, pp. 48, 51.

188. Ibid., p. 28.

189. EW, interview with John Freeman, *Face to Face*, BBC, first broadcast 9.40 p.m., 26 June 1961.

190. EW, *A Little Learning*, pp. 28, 11.

191. Douglas Lane Patey, for example, denotes Waugh's biography of Ronald Knox as the forerunner to *A Little Learning* and remarks how the former 'left the heart of the believer … largely unexamined; the book's celebrated discretion borders on impersonality.' Patey, *The Life of Evelyn Waugh*, p. 343.

192. Burgess in Stannard (ed.), *Evelyn Waugh: The Critical Heritage*, p. 471.

193. Sarel Eimerl, 'From Imp to Blimp', *The Reporter*, 3 December 1964, pp. 55–6.

194. EW, *A Little Learning*, pp. 227–8.

195. EW, 'In Which Our Hero's Fortunes Fall Very Low', *Sunday Times Weekly Review*, 26 July 1964, pp. 26, 36; p. 36.

196. Anthony Powell, *Infants of the Spring*, William Heinemann, London, 1976, p. 145.

197. Katharine Asquith to EW, 9 September 1964, from Mells Manor, Somerset; British Library, Add MS 81047.

198. EW to Katharine Asquith, 14 September 1964, cited in Amory, *The Letters of Evelyn Waugh*, p. 624.

199. Eimerl, 'From Imp to Blimp', p. 56. This sea change in awareness of sexual abuse since the 1960s is exemplified in the BBC's new adaptation of *Decline and Fall*, which does tackle the racism shown to the book's only black character but portrays Grimes merely as a philandering homosexual. There is a very slight hint towards pederasty but this is left equivocal and the boy whom it concerns is much older than either Knox minor in *A Little Learning* or Grimes's original victims in *Decline and Fall* (James Wood (writer), Matthew Bird (producer) and Guillem Morales (director), *Decline and Fall*, Tiger Aspect, first aired at 9 p.m. on 31 March 2017, BBC 1).

200. EW, *A Little Learning*, pp. 228–9.

201. Ibid., p. 206.

202. EW Diary, 15 September, 16 September 1924. Evelyn Waugh Collection 12.1.

203. EW, *A Little Learning*, p. 181.

204. Anthony Powell, *A Question of Upbringing*, William Heinemann, London, 1951, p. 229.

205. Powell, *Infants of the Spring*, p. 194.

206. See also 'The Oxford Canal', p. 105.

207. EW, 'The Balance: A Yarn of the Good Old Days of Broad Trousers and High Necked Jumpers', in Alec Waugh (ed.), *Georgian Stories, 1926*, Chapman & Hall, London, 1926, pp. 253–91; pp. 254–6.

208. Ibid., p. 277.

209. Ibid., pp. 254, 262, 263.

210. Ibid., p. 272.

211. EW Diary, 29 September 1925, Evelyn Waugh Collection 12.1–2, HRC.

212. While to modern ears this title might denote the staid and dignified, in the early twentieth century 'Georgian' was contrasted with the preceding Victorian aesthetic of realism and sentimentality to signify the innovative and iconoclastic. See Virginia Woolf, 'Mr Bennett and Mrs Brown', *The Hogarth Essays* no. 1, Hogarth Press, London, 1924.

213. Stannard, *Evelyn Waugh: Early Years*, pp. 155–6.

214. For a detailed overview of *Decline and Fall*, see Melvyn Bragg (presenter), with Ann Pasternak Slater, David Bradshaw and John Bowen, 'Decline and Fall', *In Our Time*, BBC Radio 4, first broadcast 21 February 2013, www.bbc.co.uk/programmes/b01qmbsc (accessed 21 October 2016).

215. EW, *Decline and Fall*, Chapman & Hall, London, 1928, pp. 4–7.

216. Frank Kermode, Introduction to *Decline and Fall*, *Vile Bodies* and *Put Out More Flags*, Everyman's Library, London, 2003, pp. ix–xxii; p. xxii.

217. Byrne, *Mad World*, p. 53.

218. Henry Green, *Pack My Bag: A Self Portrait* (1940), Oxford University Press, Oxford, 1989, p. 219.

219. EW, *Decline and Fall*, pp. 2–3.

220. Ibid., pp. 1–2, 6.

221. EW, *A Little Learning*, p. 167.

222. For more on this topic, see Naomi Milthorpe, 'England and the Octopus: *Decline and Fall*', in *Evelyn Waugh's Satire*, pp. 19–34.

223. EW, *Decline and Fall*, p. 6.

224. EW, 'Edward of Unique Achievement', p. 17.

225. Kermode, Introduction to *Decline and Fall*, *Vile Bodies* and *Put Out More Flags*, p. vii.

226. *The Riot Club*, directed by Lone Scherfig, Blueprint Pictures, 2014; *Posh* premiered at the Royal Court Theatre, London, 2010.

227. Catherine Shoard, 'The Riot Club Review: The PM Should Love It (and So Will Viewers)', *Guardian*, 6 September 2014, www.theguardian.com/film/2014/sep/06/the-riot-club-review-bullingdon (accessed 21 October 2016).

228. See Bragg et al., 'Decline and Fall'.

229. Kermode, Introduction to *Decline and Fall*, *Vile Bodies* and *Put Out More Flags*, pp. xiv–xv.

230. EW, *Decline and Fall*, pp. 277–8.

231. See 'Oxford: City of Invention', pp. 44–5.

232. EW, *Decline and Fall*, pp. 279, 1, 4, 284.

233. Green, *Pack My Bag*, pp. 199–204.

234. See 'Oxford: City of Memory', p. 52.

235. EW, *A Little Learning*, pp. 167, 222.

236. Ibid., p. 170.

237. Ibid., p. 167.

238. EW, *Brideshead Revisited*, p. 29.

EXPLORING WAUGH'S OXFORD

1. EW, *A Little Learning*, p. 164; Evelyn Waugh Collection 5.4 and 6.1–3, HRC.

2. EW Diary, 8 September 1945.

3. John Howard Wilson, 'A Walking Tour of Evelyn Waugh's Oxford', in Donat Gallagher, Ann Pasternak Slater and John Howard Wilson (eds), *A Handful of Mischief: New Essays on Evelyn Waugh*, Fairleigh Dickinson University Press, Lanham MD, 2011, pp. 34–61; p. 34.

4. Andrew Goudie (ed.), *Seven Hundred Years of an Oxford College: Hertford College, 1284–1984*, Hertford College, Oxford, 1999, pp. 7–9.

5. James Bettley, 'Jackson, Sir Thomas Graham, first baronet (1835–1924)', *Oxford Dictionary of National Biography*, Oxford University Press, Oxford, 2004; online edn, October 2007, www.oxforddnb.com/view/article/34140 (accessed 14 September 2016).

6. Goudie (ed.), *Seven Hundred Years*, p. 68.

7. EW, *A Little Learning*, p. 165.

8. Oxford Preservation Trust, p. 15.

9. Wilson, 'A Walking Tour', p. 35.

10. EW, *Brideshead Revisited*, pp. 27–8.

11. *Brideshead Revisited*, directed by Julian Jarrold, BBC Films, 2008.

12. Christopher Hollis, *Oxford in the Twenties: Recollections of Five Friends*, Heinemann, London, 1976, p. 83.

13. In an undated memoir about her failed marriage to Evelyn Waugh, Evelyn Gardner recalls Arthur's peculiar relish in referring to himself as a member of the lower middle classes (Evelyn Waugh Archive, Somerset).

14. Arthur Waugh, *One Man's Road*, Chapman & Hall, London, 1931, pp. 125–6.

15. EW, *A Little Learning*, p. 69.

16. Arthur Waugh, *One Man's Road*, p. 127. One such comedy was Thomas William Robertson's *School* (1869), which was not then 'out-dated with the fatal label of sentimentality'.

17. EW, *A Little Learning*, p. 69; Arthur Waugh, *One Man's Road*, pp. 318, 136.

18. EW, *A Little Learning*, pp. 154–5.

19. *The Scarlet Woman*, directed by Terence Greenidge, 1924, http://player.bfi.org.uk/film/watch-the-scarlet-woman-1924 (accessed 3 October 2016).

20. Terence Greenidge to Charles Linck, 8 October 1961, from 64 Princes Square, London; Alec Waugh Collection, HRC.

21. EW, *A Little Learning*, pp. 209–10.

22. EW, *Vile Bodies*, pp. 155–6.

23. Alexander Waugh, *Fathers and Sons*, pp. 101–2.

24. EW, *Brideshead Revisited*, p. 35.

25. EW, *A Little Learning*, p. 69.

26. Stephanie Jenkins, 'Oxford History: The High', 2014, www.oxfordhistory.org.uk/high/tour/south/092_094.html (accessed 28 June 2016).

27. EW, *A Little Learning*, pp. 146–7, 196.

28. Harold Acton, *Memoirs of an Aesthete*, Methuen, London, 1948, p. 119; Tom Driberg, *Ruling Passions*, Jonathan Cape, London, 1977, p. 56.

29. EW, *A Little Learning*, p. 213.

30. EW Diary, 18 November 1924.
31. EW Diary, 25 December 1924.
32. Yoshiharu Usui, 'Evelyn Waugh's Outfit', *Evelyn Waugh Newsletter and Studies*, vol. 39, no. 3, Winter 2009, pp. 1–8; p. 2.
33. EW Diary, 21 November 1926.
34. EW Diary, 25 February 1926.
35. EW Diary, 2 October 1926.
36. EW, *The Ordeal of Gilbert Pinfold*, p. 9.
37. 'The Weather', *The Times*, London, 23 June 1923, p. 14.
38. APGRD, 'The Rhesus (1923)', 2016, www.apgrd.ox.ac.uk/productions/production/4504 (accessed 22 September 2016).
39. EW, cover design for *The Rhesus*, OUDS, Oxford, 1923; private collection, London.
40. EW, 'Father and Son', p. 4.
41. EW Diary, 11 September 1921.
42. EW, 'Father and Son', p. 4.
43. EW Diary, 11 September 1921.
44. EW, 'Father and Son', p. 4.
45. EW, 'À Côté de Chez Todd', *A Handful of Dust*, Chapman & Hall, London, 1934, pp. 321–40.
46. Alexander Waugh, *Fathers and Sons*, pp. 226–7.
47. EW, *Brideshead Revisited*, p. 62.
48. EW, *A Little Learning*, p. 75.
49. EW, 'To Myself', dedicatory letter, [1920/1921]; Evelyn Waugh Collection 5.1–2, HRC.
50. EW, *Work Suspended: Two Chapters of an Unfinished Novel*, Chapman & Hall, London, 1942, p. 7.
51. On 26 October 1943, following a short illness, Arthur Waugh fell into a deep sleep from which he did not wake. Alexander Waugh, *Fathers and Sons*, p. 264.
52. EW, 'Father and Son', p. 5. For more on Waugh's paternal grandfather, see Alexander Waugh, 'Midsomer Norton', *Fathers and Sons*, pp. 20–46, and EW, *A Little Learning*, pp. 21–3.
53. EW Diary, [?October 1963], Evelyn Waugh Collection 13.9, HRC.
54. Wilson, 'Walking Tour', p. 47. According to Wilson, Martin Stannard and Humphrey Carpenter have the club at 34 St Aldate's, while Selina Hastings thought it was number 131.
55. Hastings, *Evelyn Waugh*, p. 90.
56. Driberg, *Ruling Passions*, pp. 47–8.
57. Ibid., p. 55.
58. The Sexual Offences Act 1967 decriminalized homosexual acts conducted in private between two males over the age of twenty-one. It applied only to England and Wales, and excluded the armed forces. www.legislation.gov.uk/ukpga/1967/60/pdfs/ukpga_19670060_en.pdf (accessed 26 October 2016).
59. EW, *A Little Learning*, p. 192.
60. Stannard, *Evelyn Waugh: The Critical Heritage*, p. 475.
61. Driberg, *Ruling Passions*, p. 49.
62. See, for example, the long-running argument in the *Evelyn Waugh Newsletter and Studies* between John Osborne and David Bittner, beginning with Osborne's 'Sebastian Flyte

as a Homosexual' (vol. 23, no. 3, Winter 1989, pp. 7–8) and Bittner's reply 'Sebastian and Charles – More Than Friends?' (vol. 24, no. 2, Autumn 1990, pp. 1–3). The debate continued for over a year. The whole back catalogue of *The Evelyn Waugh Newsletter and Studies* is available from http://leicester.contentdm.oclc.org/cdm/search/collection/p16445coll12.

63. EW, *Brideshead Revisited*, pp. 90–91.

64. Ibid., p. 225.

65. Hugh Heckstall-Smith, '"There but for the grace of God ...." ', *New Scientist*, vol. 18, no. 338, 9 May 1963, p. 335. Waugh and Heckstall-Smith had been corresponding about Waugh's Lancing mentor J.F. Roxburgh (1888–1954), himself homosexual, with whom Heckstall-Smith later taught.

66. Driberg, *Ruling Passions*, p. 49.

67. EW, *A Little Learning*, p. 203.

68. John Patrick Douglas ('Pauper') Balfour, 3rd Baron Kinross (1904–1976), became a journalist after Oxford, and was depicted as Lord Simon Balcairn in Waugh's *Vile Bodies* due to his work as 'Mr Gossip' on the *Daily Sketch* newspaper. In the 1930s Balfour and Waugh were war correspondents together in Ethiopia.

69. EW Diary, 21 June 1924, Evelyn Waugh Collection 12.1, HRC; EW, *A Little Learning*, p. 208. Waugh's diary records that he was lowered out of 'Richard's' window, and so while the two were no longer lovers they were not estranged.

70. EW, *A Little Learning*, p. 202.

71. Graham Greene to EW, 10 September 1964, from C.6 Albany, London W1; British Library, Add MS 81057.

72. Balliol had risen to pre-eminence under Benjamin Jowett (1817–1893), its master 1870–1893 and University vice-chancellor during Arthur Waugh's freshman year (1885).

73. EW, *A Little Learning*, p. 180.

74. Hastings, *Evelyn Waugh*, p. 97.

75. Waugh and Pares did stay in touch through the years, and in December 1954 Waugh wrote to Harold Acton in distress. Pares was dying of multiple sclerosis, and Waugh had been to visit his 'first love': 'quite paralysed except for his mind ... dignified ... no lolling tongue ... but ... helpless. Awaiting death with no religious comfort. A most harrowing visit' (EW to Harold Acton, 20 December 1954, from Piers Court; copy in Evelyn Waugh Archive, Somerset).

76. EW, *A Little Learning*, p. 192.

77. Lord Wicklow to EW, 16 January 1964; British Library, Add MS 81059. Wicklow only refers to 'Chris', but context suggests this was Christopher Hollis.

78. Terence Greenidge to Charles Linck, 8 October 1961.

79. *The Scarlet Woman*, directed by Terence Greenidge.

80. Powell, *Infants of the Spring*, p. 151.

81. Terence Greenidge to Charles Linck, 8 October 1961. From the cast, Terence's brother John and the OUDS star Gyles Isham also converted to Catholicism. Guy Hemingway, who played the Pope, had recently been received into the Church.

82. EW, *A Little Learning*, p. 181.

83. Lord Clonmore to EW, 16 January 1964.

84. EW, *A Little Learning*, p. 177.

85. Alexander Waugh, *Fathers and Sons*, p. 176.

86. 'Mr Loveday's Little Outing' was first published as 'Mr Crutwell's Little Outing' in the New York edition of *Harper's Bazaar* 69, March 1935, pp. 61, 130–31.

87. EW, *A Little Learning*, pp. 173–4.

88. In *A Cornishman at Oxford,* the historian A.L. Rowse remembers Cruttwell as 'an extraordinary character, with his misogyny and his idiosyncratic vocabulary. He had a Swiftian attitude and manner of speech … the ordinary female dons were "drabs", the more emotional ones "breast-heavers"' (p. 261).

89. Following the paper's serialization of *A Little Learning*, Professor M.V.C. Jeffreys wrote to the *Sunday Times* protesting that Cruttwell did his duty to all undergraduates, whether he liked them or not: the tutor's only intolerance was for the lazy. 'A Sobering Lash', 2 August 1963, p. 25.

90. C.R.M.F. Cruttwell to EW, [August 1924], from Hertford College; British Library, Add MS 81052.

91. Evelyn Gardner to John Maxse, May 1928; cited in Hastings, *Evelyn Waugh*, p. 165.

92. Alexander Waugh, *Fathers and Sons*, p. 176.

93. On p. 207 of his personal copy of *A Little Learning*, A.L. Rowse has added the marginal note: 'Cruttwell told me "I cd have sent him down".'

94. Hugh J. Compton, *The Oxford Canal*, David & Charles, Newton Abbot and London, 1976, pp. 52, 118–19. The cut was named for the Duke of Marlborough, who oversaw its opening in around 1789.

95. EW, *A Little Learning*, p. 192.

96. Ibid., pp. 188–9.

97. The earliest written version of the legend is by Joseph Glanvill and appears in *The Vanity of Dogmatizing* (c. 1661).

98. 'The Scholar-gipsy', *Poetical Works of Matthew Arnold*, Macmillan, London and New York, 1891, pp. 273–81; p. 276.

99. EW, 'The Balance', p. 289.

100. Guy Crouchback, for example, in *Men at Arms* (1952), *Officers and Gentlemen* (1955) and *Unconditional Surrender* (1961), all Chapman & Hall, London.

101. See *Scott-King's Modern Europe* (1947) and *Love Among the Ruins* (1953), both Chapman & Hall, London.

102. Basil Seal, for example, is responsible for Ambrose Silk's exile to Ireland in EW's *Put Out More Flags*, Chapman & Hall, London, 1942.

103. See EW, *Decline and Fall*, pp. 87, 121, 195.

104. See EW, *Men at Arms*, pp. 195–6.

105. The fates of *A Handful of Dust*'s Tony Last, the two anonymous victims in 'Mr Loveday's Little Outing' (*Mr Loveday's Little Outing and Other Sad Stories*, Chapman & Hall, London, 1936, pp. 7–22) and *Decline and Fall*'s Mr Prendergast are just three of many Wavian examples which fit this description.

106. Alice in Wonderland Shop, www.aliceinwonderlandshop.com (accessed 12 June 2016); Morton N. Cohen, 'Dodgson, Charles Lutwidge [Lewis Carroll] (1832–1898)', *Oxford Dictionary of National Biography*, Oxford University Press, Oxford, 2004, online edn September 2013, www.oxforddnb.com/view/article/7749 (accessed 12 June 2016); Lewis Carroll, *Alice's Adventures in Wonderland* and *Through the Looking-Glass and What Alice Found There*, Oxford University Press, Oxford, 1998, pp. 178–84.

107. Carroll, *Through the Looking-Glass*, pp. 179–80.

108. Alice in Wonderland Shop, www.aliceinwonderlandshop.com.
109. EW to Tom Driberg, [c. 18 March 1922]; SOC.Driberg W 12, Christ Church Archives, Oxford.
110. EW Diary, 23 January 1925.
111. EW, *Brideshead Revisited*, p. 29.
112. EW, *Vile Bodies*, Chapman & Hall, London, 1930, p. vii. At Lancing, EW had also used an epigraph from *Alice and Wonderland* to head a prize-winning poem about Sir Lancelot: 'Tut, Tut, child! There's a moral in everything if only you can find it.' 'Return of Lancelot after the siege of Joyous Gard', 1920, Evelyn Waugh Collection 5.1–2, HRC.
113. EW, *Vile Bodies*, p. 132.
114. *Daily Mail*, 8 October 1930, p. 12.
115. EW Diary, 10 December [1921], Evelyn Waugh Collection 3.9, HRC.
116. Christopher Hollis, *The Oxford Union*, Evans Brothers, London, 1965, pp. 260–61.
117. Ibid., p. 169.
118. EW, *A Little Learning*, p. 184.
119. Ibid.
120. Waugh's novel was torn to shreds by Ernest Oldmeadow, the editor of the Catholic weekly newspaper *The Tablet*, who declared that its sexual and blasphemous content was 'a disgrace to anybody professing the Catholic name' ('New Books and Music – to Buy or Borrow or Leave Alone', *The Tablet* 161, 7 January 1933, p. 10). A number of eminent Catholic authors wrote to defend Waugh; Oldmeadow retaliated and the row lasted for several months. The whole debate can be accessed at *The Tablet* online archive: http://archive.thetablet.co.uk/issues?year=1933#allIssues//archive.thetablet.co.uk/issues?year=1933#allIssues (accessed 26 October 2016).
121. Naomi Milthorpe, 'Collecting Material: Black Mischief, Scoop and Cold Comfort Farm', in *Evelyn Waugh's Satire*, pp. 55–79; p. 61.
122. EW, *Black Mischief*, Chapman & Hall, London, 1932, pp. 296–7.
123. Michael A.R. Graves, 'Campion, Edmund [St Edmund Campion] (1540–1581)', *Oxford Dictionary of National Biography*, Oxford University Press, Oxford, 2004; online edn, January 2008, www.oxforddnb.com/view/article/4539 (accessed 9 October 2016).
124. Stannard, *Evelyn Waugh: The Early Years*, p. 383.
125. Preface to the second American edition of EW, *Edmund Campion*, Little, Brown, Boston MA, 1946, p. ix.
126. Stannard, *Evelyn Waugh: The Early Years*, p. 388.
127. See note 120.
128. Alexander Waugh, *Fathers and Sons*, p. 217.
129. Waugh, for example, wrote in mock-bad French to Mary Lygon that he hoped the book's reception would ingratiate him with Madame Herbert, 'the mother of the lazy young girl with the huge nose'. EW to Mary Lygon, cited in Amory, *The Letters of Evelyn Waugh*, p. 106.
130. EW to Laura Herbert, [c. 27 April 1936], from Ellesmere, Salop; cited in Stannard, *Evelyn Waugh: The Early Years*, p. 420.
131. Cited in Sykes, *Evelyn Waugh*, p. 334.
132. 'I would congratulate you … if it were not for the fact that you are the outstanding writer of our generation & that recognition of this kind has been due to you for a long time. … I do feel hotly that there is not one book you have published which is not very far beyond

the books they have given the prize for up till now.' Henry Yorke [the novelist Henry Green] to EW, 18 June 1936, from 9–13 George St; British Library, Add MS 81075.

133. Stannard, *Evelyn Waugh: The Early Years*, p. 419.

134. See 'Alice's Shop', p. 109.

135. EW to Laura Herbert, [*c.* 27 April 1936].

136. Reg Little, 'Bookbinders Leaves City Centre after 125 Years', *Oxford Times*, 2008, www.oxfordtimes.co.uk/news/3822101.Bookbinders_leaves_city_centre_after_125_years (accessed 22 September 2016).

137. In 1944 Waugh remarked with annoyance that 'Maltby, the Oxford binder I have dealt with since I was an undergraduate … writes that he is too busy with "local government work" to attend to my orders.' EW Diary, 3 June 1944.

138. Little, 'Bookbinders Leaves City Centre after 125 Years'; Maltby's Bookbinders, 'Fine Binding', 2008, www.maltbysbookbinders.com/fine_bindings.htm (accessed 22 September 2016).

139. Stannard, *Evelyn Waugh: The Early Years*, p. 91.

140. EW, *A Little Learning*, pp. 93–4, 101.

141. Ibid., p. 41. Waugh's account of his childhood wonder watching shop assistants at work was originally much longer, and encapsulates his aesthetic of concision in phrases such as 'at the drapers they measured stuff on a brass yard stick let into the counter, or from the nose to the extended fingers, they nicked the edge and tore straight, they folded & wrapped & tied…'. Evelyn Waugh Collection 5.4 and 6.1–3, HRC.

142. Alan Pryce-Jones, review of *A Little Learning* in *New York Herald Tribune*, 3 November 1964, p. 19.

143. EW, *A Little Learning*, p. 139.

144. For example, when *Basil Seal Rides Again* was published in 1963 Waugh wrote to Nancy Mitford hoping that Seal's claim to have fathered his daughter's fiancé was obviously 'totally false' (EW to Nancy Mitford, 29 October 1963, from Combe Florey; cited in Mosley (ed.), *The Letters of Nancy Mitford and Evelyn Waugh*, p. 488). See 'Oxford: City of Memory', pp. 49–50, for a discussion of Waugh's 1959 preface to *Brideshead Revisited*.

145. EW, *Unconditional Surrender*, pp. 310–11.

146. See Jeffrey Manley, 'Guy's Deleted Nippers: War Trilogy Variant Endings Persist and Proliferate', paper at 'Evelyn Waugh and his Circle' international conference, Leicester, 2015, https://soundcloud.com/artshumlaw/martin-stannard-donat-gallagher-jeff-manley-textual-editing-panel (accessed 26 October 2016).

147. For an in-depth discussion of the mechanics of lexical mis- and displacement in these novels, see Naomi Milthorpe, 'Collecting Material: *Black Mischief*, *Scoop* and *Cold Comfort Farm*', in *Evelyn Waugh's Satire*, pp. 55–79.

148. EW, *Officers and Gentlemen*, Chapman & Hall, London, 1955, p. 255.

149. Keith Thomas, 'College Life, 1945–1970', in Brian Harrison (ed.), *A History of the University of Oxford*, Volume II: *The Twentieth Century*, Clarendon Press, Oxford, 1994, pp. 189–215; p. 201.

150. EW to A.D. Peters, 11 July 1962, from Combe Florey; A.D. Peters Collection, HRC.

151. EW, *A Little Learning*, p. 193.

152. *Brideshead Revisited* bound holograph with author revisions, 1944, 200 pages, including undated 'Ms interpolations in second draft', holograph with author paste-ins, n.d., 25 pages, Evelyn Waugh Collection 1.7, HRC.

153. EW, *A Little Learning*, p. 193.

154. 'The Union', *Isis*, 8 February 1922, p. 12; EW, *A Little Learning*, p. 191.

155. EW, *Labels*, pp. 21–2.

156. EW, *Brideshead Revisited*, p. 92.

157. EW, *A Little Learning*, pp. 214–16.

158. Patey, *Evelyn Waugh*, p. 342.

159. Gwen Plunket-Greene to EW, 12 November 1958; British Library, Add MS 81058.

160. EW, *A Little Learning*, p. 218.

161. EW, *Brideshead Revisited*, pp. 270–71

162. A.L. Rowse's personal copy of *Brideshead Revisited*, p. 128.

163. EW, *A Little Learning*, pp. 202–3.

164. EW, *Put Out More Flags*, pp. 186–8.

165. EW, *Frankly Speaking*.

166. Hastings, *Evelyn Waugh*, p. 91.

167. Hollis, *Oxford in the Twenties*, p. 76.

168. Hastings, *Evelyn Waugh*, p. 561.

169. EW to Ann Fleming, 3 March 1964, from Combe Florey; cited in Amory (ed.), *The Letters of Evelyn Waugh*, p. 618.

170. *Daily Express*, 20 October 1930, p. 10.

171. EW, *Brideshead Revisited*, p. 271

172. In 1923 there was a second station in Oxford, on the site now occupied by the Said Business School. That station was run by the London and North Western Railway. See Vic Mitchell and Keith Smith, *Oxford to Bletchley*, Middleton Press, Midhurst, 2005.

173. Signed five-shilling dinner menu for 28 November 1923, Penzance–Aberdeen Service, Great Western Railway, Evelyn Waugh Collection uncategorized material, HRC.

174. EW, *A Little Learning*, p. 194.

175. Ibid., p. 183. The writer John Buchan had been an earlier member of the White Rose: 'we drank to the King over the Water without a notion of what we meant. I remember my surprise in 1915 in Flanders when I found that Prince Rupprecht of Bavaria, the commander opposite us, was the gentleman whom we had been wont to salute by telegram on his birthday as Prince Robert of Wales!' *Memory Hold-the-Door*, Hodder & Stoughton, London, 1940, p. 55.

176. EW, *A Little Learning*, p. 195.

177. EW to John Sutro, 20 November 1963; Bodleian Library, Oxford, MS. Eng. c. 7256, fols 83–115.

178. EW to John Sutro, 22 October 1963; Bodleian Library, Oxford, MS. Eng. c. 7256, fols 83–115.

179. EW to Alfred Duggan, 18 November 1963; cited in Amory (ed.), *The Letters of Evelyn Waugh*, pp. 615–16.

180. EW Diary, 14 November 1963.

181. 'Basil Seal Rides Again' (part one), *Sunday Telegraph*, 10 February 1963, pp. 4–5; p. 5.

182. I.e. in *Black Mischief* (1930) and *Put Out More Flags* (1942).

183. EW Diary, 14 November 1963.

184. Wilson, 'Walking Tour', p. 47.

185. English Heritage and Crown Copyright, 'The Old Palace, Bishop Kings Palace, Oxford',

1954, www.britishlistedbuildings.co.uk/en-245771–the-old-palace-bishop-kings-palace-oxfor#.waeysxq4tww (accessed 14 October 2016).

186. Stephanie Jenkins, 'Old Oxford: St Aldate's, Bishop King's Palace', 2014, www.oxfor-dhistory.org.uk/old_oxford/st_aldates/bishops_palace.html (accessed 14 October 2016). There is no evidence that Bishop King actually lived in the palace.

187. Sheridan Gilley, 'Knox, Ronald Arbuthnott (1888–1957)', *Oxford Dictionary of National Biography*, Oxford University Press, Oxford, 2004; online edn, April 2016, www.oxforddnb.com/view/article/34358 (accessed 14 October 2016).

188. Patey, *Evelyn Waugh*, p. 341.

189. Stannard, *Evelyn Waugh: The Early Years*, p. 386. See also 'St John's College and Campion Hall', pp. 114–17.

190. Gilley, 'Knox', n.pag.

191. EW, *The Life of Right Reverend Ronald Knox*, Chapman & Hall, 1959, p. 272.

192. EW, Officers and Gentlemen, Chapman & Hall, London, 1955, p. 255. Stannard, *Evelyn Waugh: No Abiding City*, pp. 402, 91.

193. Waugh's wife Laura was hopeless in this regard. Waugh had to beg her, repeatedly, for comment on *Brideshead Revisited*: 'Can you not see how it disappoints me that this book, which I … have dedicated to you, should have no comment … [?]' This letter crossed with a paragraph from Laura about possible conflicts with Catholic doctrine and featuring the tortured sign-off: 'I love you & admire you heartily' (EW to Laura Waugh, 7 January 1945, from 37 Military Mission, [Dubrovnik]; cited in Amory (ed.), *The Letters of Evelyn Waugh*, p. 195; Laura Waugh to EW, 26 December 1944, British Library, Add MS 81073).

194. Stannard, *Evelyn Waugh: No Abiding City*, pp. 129–30, 157, 305.

195. Patey, *Evelyn Waugh*, p. 341.

196. Knox and Lady Acton had what has been described as a 'platonic love affair'. He was the single largest influence on her conversion to Catholicism, and in 1938 retired from Oxford to the Acton family home, Aldenham Park. He lived there for nearly a decade before the Actons emigrated to Rhodesia in 1947. Gilley, 'Knox', n.pag.

197. EW to Daphne Acton, 20 October 1959, from Combe Florey; cited in Amory (ed.), *The Letters of Evelyn Waugh*, pp. 529–30.

198. Stannard, *Evelyn Waugh: The Early Years*, p. 388; Patey, *Evelyn Waugh*, p. 341.

199. The information in the following two paragraphs is drawn from pp. 3–8 of *A Brief History of Christ Church*, which is published online by the College and available from www.chch.ox.ac.uk/sites/default/files/Brief-History-2016rev.pdf (accessed 21 October 2016). The compilers cite J.F.A. Mason's entry on Christ Church in Christopher Hibbert (ed.), *The Encyclopaedia of Oxford*, Macmillan, London, 1988, as their principal source.

200. EW, *A Little Learning*, p. 198.

201. Marginal note in A.L. Rowse's personal copy of *A Little Learning*, p. 205.

202. Rowse, *A Cornishman at Oxford*, p. 20.

203. *A Brief History of Christ Church*, p. 10.

204. Ibid.; EW, *Brideshead Revisited*, pp. 43, 45, 46.

205. Christ Church, 'The Cathedral', 2016, www.chch.ox.ac.uk/visiting-christ-church/cathedral (accessed 21 October 2016).

206. EW, *Brideshead Revisited*, p. 31.

207. Sebastian might be referring to the Danby Gateway, built by Inigo Jones's master sculptor Nicholas Stone and completed in 1633 (Mavis Batey, *Oxford Gardens: The University's*

Influence on Garden History, Avebury, Amersham, 1982, pp. 32–3). If so, appreciation of the archway would be a prelude to Charles's 'conversion to the baroque' which occurs at Brideshead Castle (EW, *Brideshead Revisited*, p. 73).

208. EW, *A Little Learning*, p. 154.

209. Susannah Gibson, 'Vegetable: The Creation of New Life'. *Animal, Vegetable or Mineral? How Eighteenth-Century Science Disrupted the Natural Order*, Oxford University Press, Oxford, 2015, pp. 79–116; pp. 79–82.

210. See, for example, Arthur O. Lovejoy's *The Great Chain of Being: A Study of the History of an Idea*, Harvard University Press, Cambridge MA and London, 1936 and 1964.

211. See, for example, EW's 'The Same Again Please', *Spectator*, 23 November 1962, one of some seventeen articles and letters he wrote during 1962–64 objecting to the recommendations of Vatican II.

212. EW, 'Out of Depth', *Mr Loveday's Little Outing and Other Sad Stories*, pp. 119–38; p. 136.

213. Batey, *Oxford Gardens*, pp. 31–2.

214. Thomas Coghan, *The Haven of Health*, London, 1584, pp. 3–4; cited in Nicholas Richardson, 'The Chapel Tennis Balls', in Stephen Gunn (ed.), *Treasures of Merton College*, Third Millennium Publishing, London, 2013, pp. 66–7; p. 67.

215. Richardson, 'The Chapel Tennis Balls', p. 67.

216. EW, *A Little Learning*, p. 207. This is the third time *A Little Learning* employs the phrase in connection with Oxford, suggesting that Waugh might have given himself up to 'pure pleasure' quite a while before his projected final term.

217. EW, *A Little Learning*, p. 167.

218. Byrne, *Mad World*, pp. 62–3.

219. In his personal copy of *A Little Learning* A.L. Rowse, himself gay, cheerfully annotated his margins with 'Ho' by the names of those he considered homosexual and identified both Richard Pares and Hugh Lygon as Waugh's lovers. He also recorded his own escape from Waugh's lecherous friend Brian Howard: 'his long eye-lashes once appraised, and dismissed me: not his type, which was rough stuff' (pp. 107, 181, 205).

220. Byrne, *Mad World*, p. 44.

221. Dorothy Lygon to EW, 25 February 1945, from RAF HQ 336 Wing; British Library, Add MS 81061.

222. Stannard, *Evelyn Waugh: The Early Years*, p. 285.

223. Byrne, *Mad World*, pp. 156–9.

224. Alexander Glen, *Young Men in the Arctic: The Oxford University Arctic Expedition to Spitsbergen, 1933*, Faber & Faber, London, 1935, pp. 243–4.

225. EW, 'The First Time I Went to the North: Fiasco in the Arctic', in Theodora Benson (ed.), *The First Time I ...*, Chapman & Hall, London, 1935, pp. 149–62; p. 160.

226. Byrne, *Mad World*, pp. 233–4.

227. Ibid., pp. 254–5.

228. Telegram from Lady Mary ('Maimie') Lygon to EW, 21 November 1939, postmarked Dulverton, Somerset; British Library, Add MS 81061.

229. Byrne, *Mad World*, p. 176.

Bibliography

WORKS BY EVELYN WAUGH

Only works cited in the book appear in the bibliography. Please refer to 'Evelyn Waugh's Life and Works' (pp. xiv–xvii) for a full list of Waugh's publications.

First editions & printings

'Portrait of Young Man With Career', *Isis*, 30 May 1923, p. xxii.

'Anthony, Who Sought Things That Were Lost', *Oxford Broom*, vol. 1, no. 3, June 1923, pp. 14–20.

'Edward of Unique Achievement', *Cherwell*, 1 August 1923, pp. 14, 16–18.

'The Balance: A Yarn of the Good Old Days of Broad Trousers and High Necked Jumpers', in A. Waugh (ed.), *Georgian Stories, 1926*, Chapman & Hall, London, 1926, pp. 253–91.

Decline and Fall, Chapman & Hall, London, 1928.

Vile Bodies, Chapman & Hall, London, 1930.

Labels: A Mediterranean Journal, Duckworth, London, 1930.

Black Mischief, Chapman & Hall, London, 1932.

Ninety-Two Days, Duckworth, London, 1934.

A Handful of Dust, Chapman & Hall, London, 1934.

'Mr Crutwell's Little Outing', *Harper's Bazaar* (New York edn) 69, March 1935, pp. 61, 130–31.

Waugh in Abyssinia, Longmans, London, 1936.

Put Out More Flags, Chapman & Hall, London, 1942.

Work Suspended: Two Chapters of an Unfinished Novel, Chapman & Hall, London, 1942.

Brideshead Revisited, Chapman & Hall, London, 1945.

'St. Helena Meets Constantius: A Legend Retold', *The Tablet*, vol. 186, no. 5511, 22 December 1945, pp. 7–10.

Scott-King's Modern Europe, Chapman & Hall, London, 1947.

'Compassion', *Month* NS 2, August 1949, pp. 79–98.

Men at Arms, Chapman & Hall, London, 1952.

Love Among the Ruins, Chapman & Hall, London, 1953.

Officers and Gentlemen, Chapman & Hall, London, 1955.

The Ordeal of Gilbert Pinfold, Chapman & Hall, London, 1957.

The Life of Right Reverend Ronald Knox, Chapman & Hall, London, 1959.

Unconditional Surrender, Chapman & Hall, London, 1961.

'Basil Seal Rides Again' (part one), *Sunday Telegraph*, 10 February 1963.
A Little Learning, Chapman & Hall, London, 1964.

Other editions

Brideshead Revisited, Uniform Edition (1960), Penguin Classics, London, 2011.
Decline and Fall, *Vile Bodies* and *Put Out More Flags*, Everyman's Library, London, 2003, with an introduction by Frank Kermode, pp. ix–xxii.
Edmund Campion, 2nd American edn, Little, Brown, Boston MA, 1946.
A Little Learning, Little, Brown, Boston MA and Toronto, 1964.
A Little Learning, ed. B. Cooke and J.H. Wilson, Oxford University Press, Oxford, 2017.
Vile Bodies, Uniform Edition, Chapman & Hall, London, 1965.

Articles

'The Youngest Generation', *Lancing College Magazine*, December 1921, p. 85.
'Come to Keble', *Isis*, 21 February 1923, p. 7 (unsigned).
'Seen in the Dark', *Isis*, 23 January 1924, p. 5.
'Seen in the Dark: The Oxford Super Cinema', *Isis*, 30 January 1924, p. 6.
'Wittenberg and Oxford', *Isis*, 14 February 1924, pp. 1–2.
'Isis Idol No. 594; Mr Harold Acton (Christ Church), Editor of *The Oxford Broom*, Author of *Aquarium* etc.', *Isis*, 20 February 1924, p. 17 (unsigned).
'My Favourite Film Star', *Daily Mail*, 24 May 1930, p. 10.
'Let the Marriage Vow Mean Something', *Daily Mail*, 8 October 1930, p. 12.
'Converted to Rome: Why It Has Happened to Me', *Daily Express*, 20 October 1930, p. 10.
'The First Time I Went to the North: Fiasco in the Arctic', in Theodora Benson (ed.), *The First Time I ...*, Chapman & Hall, London, 1935, pp. 149–62.
'The Same Again Please', *Spectator*, 23 November 1962, pp. 11–14.
'Father and Son', *Sunday Telegraph*, 2 December 1962, pp. 4–5.

Illustrations

'At the Sign of the Unicorn', *Cherwell*, 7 March 1923, p. 6.
'Bertram, Ludovic and Ann', *Isis*, 24 May 1923, p.23. Graphic art with open letter.
Title page, *Cherwell*, 1 August 1923 and thereafter until 1929. Five Oxford 'types' depicted as marionettes.
'Youth', *London Mercury* 8, October 1923, p. 635. Wood engraving of a young man with one foot in the cradle and one in the grave.
'The Seven Deadly Sins. No III. The Wanton Way of Those that Corrupt the Very Young', *Cherwell*, 3 November 1923, p. 32. To accompany poem signed 'M.C.H.'
Man and woman in period dress on a half-canopied bed (p. 26), a satyr seated (p. 39), and two men (p. 43), in C. Bax (ed.), *The Golden Hind*, vol. 2, no. 6, Chapman & Hall, London, January 1924.
'Cornish Landscape with White Cow in Thought. E.W. 1924', *Cherwell*, 2 February 1924, p. 40.

Interviews

Frankly Speaking, BBC Home Service, first broadcast 10.05–10.35 p.m., 16 November 1953. Interview with Stephen Black, Jack Davies and Charles Wilmot.
Face to Face, BBC, first broadcast 9.40 p.m., 26 June 1961. Interview with John Freeman.

ARCHIVAL COLLECTIONS

Harry Ransom Center, Austin, Texas

A.D. Peters Collection

Letter from Evelyn Waugh to A.D. Peters, 11 July 1962, from Combe Florey.

Alec Waugh Collection

Letter from Alec Waugh to Arthur and Catherine Waugh, 6 December 1908, from Fernden School.
Letter from A.H. Trelawny Ross to Alec Waugh, 2 January 1918, from Devonport.
Letter from Terence Greenidge to Charles Linck, 8 October 1961, from 64 Princes Square, London.

Evelyn Waugh Collection

Waugh, E., 'To Myself', dedicatory letter, [1920/1921], Box 5 Folders 1–2.
Waugh, E., 'Return of Lancelot after the siege of Joyous Gard', 1920, Box 5 Folders 1–2.
Signed five-shilling dinner menu for 28 November 1923, Penzance–Aberdeen Service, Great Western Railway, uncategorized material.
Waugh, E., *Brideshead Revisited* bound holograph with author revisions, 1944, 200 pages, including undated 'Ms interpolations in second draft', holograph with author paste-ins, n.d., 25 pages, Box 1 Folder 7.
Waugh, E., *A Little Learning*, loose manuscript and typescript pages, 1961–63, Box 5 Folder 4 and Box 6 Folders 1–3.

Evelyn Waugh Diaries

1911–12   Box 3 Folder 2
1914   Box 3 Folder 6
1914–16   Box 3 Folder 7
1916   Box 3 Folder 8
1919–21   Box 3 Folders 9–10
1924–25   Box 12 Folder 1
1925–26   Box 12 Folder 2
1926–27   Box 12 Folder 3
1927   Box 12 Folder 4
1943–44   Box 12 Folders 14–15
1944–45   Box 12 Folder 16
1945–46   Box 13 Folder 1
1960–65   Box 13 Folder 9

Leeds University Library, Leeds

Fay and Geoffrey Elliot Collection

Waugh, E. (ed)., *The Pistol Troop magazine*. Volume 1. Carbon typescript with autograph manuscript title-page. 1912. Boxed with this item are three programmes for plays performed at the Waugh family home: *Feed the Brute*, *The Man From Downing St* and *Beauty and the Beast* (performed January 1912). This copy probably belonged to Max Fleming.
Waugh, E., *A Little Learning*, Chapman & Hall, London, 1964. A.L. Rowse's copy with his manuscript annotations, mostly critical of Waugh, but at times unexpectedly appreciative of his talent.

British Library, London
Evelyn Waugh Papers
Letter from Richard Pares to Evelyn Waugh, [?1923], from Westfield, Surbiton. Add MS 81068.
Letter from C.R.M.F. Cruttwell to Evelyn Waugh, [August 1924], from Hertford College. Add MS 81052.
Letter from Henry Yorke [Henry Green] to Evelyn Waugh, 18 June 1936, from 9–13 George St. Add MS 81075.
Telegram from Lady Mary ('Maimie') Lygon to Evelyn Waugh, 21 November 1939, postmarked Dulverton, Somerset. Add MS 81061.
Nancy Mitford to Evelyn Waugh, 22 December 1944. Add MS 81064.
Letter from Laura Waugh to Evelyn Waugh, 26 December 1944. Add MS 81073.
Letter from Dorothy Lygon to Evelyn Waugh, 25 February 1945, from RAF HQ 336 Wing. Add MS 81061.
Letter from Gwen Plunket-Greene to Evelyn Waugh, 12 November 1958. Add MS 81058.
Letter from John MacDougall to Evelyn Waugh, 25 February 1963. Add MS 81062.
Letter from Gerald Gardiner to Evelyn Waugh, 3 August 1963, from 12 King's Bench Walk. Add MS 81057.
Letter from John Sutro to Evelyn Waugh, 3 August 1963, from 26 Belgrave Square, London SW1. Add MS 81070.
Letter from Lord Wicklow to Evelyn Waugh, 16 January 1964. Add MS 81059.
Letter from Graham Greene to Evelyn Waugh, 10 September 1964, from C.6 Albany, London W1. Add MS 81057.

Bodleian Library, Oxford
MS. Eng. c. 7256, fols 83–115.
Letter from Evelyn Waugh to John Sutro, 6 August 1963.
Letter from Evelyn Waugh to John Sutro, 20 November 1963.
Letter from Evelyn Waugh to John Sutro, 22 October 1963.

Christ Church, Oxford
Letter from Evelyn Waugh to Tom Driberg [c. 18 March 1922]. SOC.Driberg W 12.

Huntington Library, Pasadena
Evelyn Waugh Papers
Letter from Evelyn Waugh to Gillon Aitken, 29 January 1964. 7.230.

Evelyn Waugh Archive, Somerset
Letter from Evelyn Waugh to Teresa Jungman, 14 November 1931, from Easton Court, Chagford.
Letter from Evelyn Waugh to Laura Waugh, [c. 23 March] 1944.
Copy of letter from Evelyn Waugh to Desmond MacCarthy, 27 July 1945.
Copy of letter from Evelyn Waugh to Harold Acton, 20 December 1954, from Piers Court.
Letter from Evelyn Waugh to Randolph Churchill, 18 September 1964, from Combe Florey.
Undated memoir by Evelyn Nightingale (née Gardner) about her childhood and failed marriage to Evelyn Waugh.

Georgetown University Library, Washington DC
Christopher Sykes Collection
Postcard from Evelyn Waugh to Christopher Sykes, [c. 21 September] 1964, from Combe Florey. 13.14.
Letter from Harman Grisewood to Christopher Sykes, 2 April 1973. 5.30.

PRIVATE COLLECTIONS
Nicholas Shakespeare Collection
Dudley Carew diary, 15 December 1921, Oxford.

Oxford Preservation Trust
Letter from Evelyn Waugh printed in the matinée souvenir programme for the New Theatre, Oxford, 28 February 1930, p. 15.

Anonymous
Bookplate for Alastair Graham featuring a faun perched on a ruined column [c. 1924]. Leicester.
Cover design for *The Rhesus*, OUDS, Oxford, 1923. London.
Letter from Evelyn Waugh to Margaret Waugh, October 1962. Somerset.

BIOGRAPHIES OF EVELYN WAUGH

Eade, P., *Evelyn Waugh: A Life Revisited*, Orion, London, 2016.
Hastings, S., *Evelyn Waugh: A Biography*, Minerva, London, 1995.
Hollis, C., *Oxford in the Twenties: Recollections of Five Friends*, Heinemann, London, 1976.
Stannard, M., *Evelyn Waugh: The Early Years, 1903–1939*, J.M. Dent, London, 1986.
Stannard, M., *Evelyn Waugh: No Abiding City, 1939–1966*, J.M. Dent, London, 1992.
Sykes, C., *Evelyn Waugh: A Biography*, HarperCollins, London, 1975.
Waugh, Alec, *My Brother Evelyn and Other Profiles*, Cassell, London, 1967.
Waugh, Alexander, *Fathers and Sons*, Broadway, New York, 2007.

BOOKS, POEMS, CHAPTERS, WEBSITES & ARTICLES

Acton, H., *Memoirs of an Aesthete*, Methuen, London, 1948.
Alberge, D., 'Lost Evelyn Waugh Letters Reveal Thwarted Love for "Bright Young Thing"', *Observer*, 21 July 2013, www.theguardian.com/books/2013/jul/21/evelyn-waugh-love-letters (accessed September 2016).
Alice in Wonderland Shop, www.aliceinwonderlandshop.com (accessed 12 June 2016).
Amory, M. (ed.), *The Letters of Evelyn Waugh*, Weidenfeld & Nicolson, London, 1980.
APGRD, 'The Rhesus (1923)', 2016, www.apgrd.ox.ac.uk/productions/production/4504 (accessed 22 September 2016).
Arnold, M., 'The Scholar-gipsy', *Poetical Works of Matthew Arnold*, Macmillan, London and New York, 1891, pp. 273–81.
Batey, M., *Oxford Gardens: The University's Influence on Garden History*, Avebury, Amersham, 1982.

Bedford, S., 'The Loved and Loving One', *New York Herald Tribune Book Week* 15, November 1964, pp. 3, 25.

Beevor, A., *Crete: The Battle and the Resistance*, John Murray, London, 1991.

Belloc, H., 'To the Balliol Men Still in Africa', *Verses*, with an introduction by Joyce Kilmer, Laurence J. Gomme, New York, 1916, pp. 28–9.

Bettley, J., 'Jackson, Sir Thomas Graham, first baronet (1835–1924)', *Oxford Dictionary of National Biography*, Oxford University Press, Oxford, 2004; online edn, October 2007, www.oxforddnb. com/view/article/34140 (accessed 14 September 2016).

Bittner, D., 'Sebastian and Charles – More Than Friends?', *Evelyn Waugh Newsletter and Studies*, vol. 24, no. 2, Autumn 1990, pp. 1–3, http://leicester.contentdm.oclc.org/cdm/compoundobject/ collection/p16445coll12/id/708/rec/2 (accessed 26 October 2016).

A Brief History of Christ Church, 2016, www.chch.ox.ac.uk/sites/default/files/Brief-History-2016rev. pdf (accessed 21 October 2016).

Buchan, J., *Memory Hold-the-Door*, Hodder & Stoughton, London, 1940.

Burgess, A., 'Waugh Begins', *Encounter*, December 1964, pp. 64, 66, 68.

Byrne, P., *Mad World: Evelyn Waugh and the Secrets of Brideshead*, Harper Press, London, 2009.

Cabell, J.B., *Jurgen, A Comedy of Justice*, Robert M. McBride, New York, 1919.

Carroll, L. *Alice's Adventures in Wonderland* and *Through the Looking-Glass and What Alice Found There*, Oxford University Press, Oxford, 1998.

Charques, R.D., Review of *Helena* in the *Spectator*, vol. 184, no. 6381, 13 October 1950, p. 12.

Christ Church, 'The Cathedral', www.chch.ox.ac.uk/visiting-christ-church/cathedral (accessed 21 October 2016).

Cockburn, C., *In a Time of Trouble: An Autobiography*, Rupert Hart-Davis, London, 1956.

Coghan, T., *The Haven of Health*, n.p., London, 1584.

Cohen, M.N., 'Dodgson, Charles Lutwidge [Lewis Carroll] (1832–1898)', *Oxford Dictionary of National Biography*, Oxford University Press, Oxford, 2004; online edn, September 2013, www. oxforddnb.com/view/article/7749 (accessed 12 June 2016).

Compton, H.J., *The Oxford Canal*, David & Charles, Newton Abbot and London, 1976.

Cooper, A. (ed.), *Mr Wu and Mrs Stitch: The Letters of Evelyn Waugh and Diana Cooper*, Hodder & Stoughton, London, 1991.

Davis, R.M., P.A. Doyle, D. Gallagher, C.E. Linck and W.M. Bogaards, *A Bibliography of Evelyn Waugh*, 2nd edn, Whitston, New York, 1986.

Doyle, P.A., Review of *A Little Learning* in *Best Sellers* 24, 15 November 1964, p. 322.

Driberg, T., *Ruling Passions*, Jonathan Cape, London, 1977.

Dulac, E., *Edmund Dulac's Fairy-Book: Fairy Tales of the Allied Nations,* Hodder & Stoughton, London, 1916.

Eimerl, S., 'From Imp to Blimp', *The Reporter*, 3 December 1964, pp. 55–6.

English Heritage and Crown Copyright, 'The Old Palace, Bishop Kings Palace, Oxford', 1954, www.britishlistedbuildings.co.uk/en-245771–the-old-palace-bishop-kings-palace-oxfor#. WAEySxQ4Tww (accessed 14 October 2016).

Fowle, F., 'Cover Design for the "Yellow Book"', 2000, www.tate.org.uk/art/artworks/beardsley-cover-design-for-the-yellow-book-n04171/text-summary (accessed 1 October 2016).

Gallagher, D., and C. Villar Flor, *In the Picture: The Facts Behind the Fiction in Evelyn Waugh's* 'Sword of Honour', Rodopi, Amsterdam and New York, 2014.

Gibson, S., 'Vegetable: The Creation of New Life', in *Animal, Vegetable or Mineral? How Eighteenth-Century Science Disrupted the Natural Order*, Oxford University Press, Oxford, 2015, pp. 79–116.

Gilley, S., 'Knox, Ronald Arbuthnott (1888–1957)', *Oxford Dictionary of National Biography*, Oxford University Press, Oxford, 2004; online edn, April 2016, www.oxforddnb.com/view/article/34358 (accessed 14 October 2016).

Glanvill, J., *The Vanity of Dogmatizing*, n.p. [*c.* 1661]. Glen, A., *Young Men in the Arctic: The Oxford University Arctic Expedition to Spitsbergen, 1933*, Faber & Faber, London, 1935.

Goudie, A. (ed.), *Seven Hundred Years of an Oxford College: Hertford College, 1284–1984*, Hertford College, Oxford, 1999.

Graves, M.A.R., 'Campion, Edmund [St Edmund Campion] (1540–1581)', *Oxford Dictionary of National Biography*, Oxford University Press, Oxford, 2004; online edn, January 2008, www.oxforddnb.com/view/article/4539, (accessed 9 October 2016).

Green, H., *Pack My Bag: A Self Portrait* (1940), Oxford University Press, Oxford, 1989.

Gross, J., 'Waugh Revisited', *New York Review of Books* 3, 13 December 1964, pp. 4–5.

Heckstall-Smith, H., '"There but for the grace of God…"', *New Scientist*, vol. 18, no. 338, 9 May 1963, p. 335.

Heyne, P.T., 'To Thine Own Self Be True', *Cresset* 28, January 1965, pp. 24–5.

Hibbert, C., (ed.), *The Encyclopaedia of Oxford*, Macmillan, London, 1988.

Hollis, C., *The Oxford Union*, Evans Brothers, London, 1965.

Jeffreys, M.V.C., 'A Sobering Lash', *Sunday Times*, 2 August 1963, p. 25.

Jenkins, S., 'Old Oxford: St Aldate's, Bishop King's Palace', 2014, www.oxfordhistory.org.uk/old_oxford/st_aldates/bishops_palace.html (accessed 14 October 2016).

Jenkins, S., 'Oxford History: The High', 2014, www.oxfordhistory.org.uk/high/tour/south/092_094.html (accessed 28 June 2016).

Little, R., 'Bookbinders Leaves City Centre after 125 Years', *Oxford Times*, 2008, www.oxfordtimes.co.uk/news/3822101.Bookbinders_leaves_city_centre_after_125_years (accessed 22 September 2016).

Lovejoy, A.O., *The Great Chain of Being: A Study of the History of an Idea*, Harvard University Press, Cambridge MA and London, 1936 and 1964.

Mackenzie, C., *Sinister Street*, vols 1–2, Martin Secker, London, 1913–14.

Maltby's Bookbinders, 'Fine Binding', 2008, www.maltbysbookbinders.com/fine_bindings.htm (accessed 22 September 2016).

Milthorpe, N., *Evelyn Waugh's Satire: Texts and Contexts*, Farleigh Dickinson University Press, Lanham MD and London, 2016.

Mitchell, V., and K. Smith, *Oxford to Bletchley*, Middleton Press, Midhurst, 2005.

Molt, C.C., and E.M. Molt, *Clent's Way*, Chapman & Hall, London, 1923.

Mosley, C. (ed.), *The Letters of Nancy Mitford and Evelyn Waugh*, Penguin Modern Classics, London, 2010.

Oldmeadow, E., 'New Books and Music – to Buy or Borrow or Leave Alone', *The Tablet* 161, 7 January 1933, p. 10 (unsigned), http://archive.thetablet.co.uk/page/7th-january-1933/10 (accessed 26 October 2016).

Osborne, J., 'Sebastian Flyte as a Homosexual', *Evelyn Waugh Newsletter and Studies*, vol. 23, no. 3, Winter 1989, pp. 7–8, http://leicester.contentdm.oclc.org/cdm/compoundobject/collection/p16445coll12/id/690/rec/1 (accessed 26 October 2016).

Petrie, C., 'An Author's Yesterday', *Illustrated London News* 245, 3 October 1964, p. 503.

Plomer, W., Review of *A Little Learning* in *The Listener*, 10 September 1964, p. 397.

Poe, E.A., *The Bells and Other Poems*, Hodder & Stoughton, London, New York and Toronto, 1912.

Powell, D., 'What Every Woman Thinks', *Isis*, 4 June 1924, p. 13.

Pritchett, V.S., 'Mr. Waugh's Exile', *New Statesman* 68, 25 September 1964, pp. 445–6.

Quennell, P., 'A Kingdom of Cokayne', in D. Pryce-Jones (ed.), *Evelyn Waugh and His World*, Weidenfeld & Nicolson, London, 1973.

Richardson, N., 'The Chapel Tennis Balls', in S. Gunn (ed.), *Treasures of Merton College*, Third Millennium Publishing, London, 2013, pp. 66–7.

Rowse, A.L., *A Cornishman at Oxford*, Jonathan Cape, London, 1965.

The Sexual Offences Act, www.legislation.gov.uk/ukpga/1967/60/pdfs/ukpga_19670060_en.pdf (accessed 26 October 2016).

Shaw, M., 'Children's Animal Tales', British Library Articles, www.bl.uk/animal-tales/articles/childrens-animal-tales (accessed 4 October 2016).

Shoard, C., 'The Riot Club Review: The PM Should Love It (and So Will Viewers)', *Guardian*, 6 September 2014, www.theguardian.com/film/2014/sep/06/the-riot-club-review-bullingdon (accessed 21 October 2016).

Stannard, M. (ed.), *Evelyn Waugh: The Critical Heritage*, Routledge & Kegan Paul, London, 1984.

Thomas, K., 'College Life, 1945–1970', in B. Harrison (ed.), *A History of the University of Oxford*, Volume II: *The Twentieth Century*, Clarendon Press, Oxford, 1994.

'The Union', *Isis*, 8 February 1922, p. 12.

Usui, Y., 'Evelyn Waugh's Outfit', *Evelyn Waugh Newsletter and Studies*, vol. 39, no. 3, Winter 2009, pp. 1–8.

Waife, G., *Colleagues*, Chapman & Hall, London, 1923.

Waugh, Alec, *The Loom of Youth*, Richard's Press, London, 1917.

Waugh, Alec, *The Early Years of Alec Waugh*, Cassell, London, 1962.

Waugh, Alec, *Best Wine Last*, W.H. Allen, London, 1978.

Waugh, Arthur, 'On Reticence in Literature', in E. Mathews and J. Lane (eds), *The Yellow Book: An Illustrated Quarterly* 1, published in London by E. Mathews & J. Lane and in Boston MA by Copeland & Day, April 1894, pp. 201–19.

Waugh, Arthur, *One Man's Road*, Chapman & Hall, London, 1931.

'The Weather', *The Times*, London, 23 June 1923, p. 14.

Wilson, E., 'Splendors and Miseries of Evelyn Waugh', *New Yorker* 21, 5 January 1946, pp. 71–4.

Wilson, J.H., 'A Walking Tour of Evelyn Waugh's Oxford', in D. Gallagher, A. Pasternak Slater and J.H. Wilson (eds), *A Handful of Mischief: New Essays on Evelyn Waugh*, Fairleigh Dickinson University Press, Lanham MD, 2011, pp. 34–61.

Woolf, V., 'Mr Bennett and Mrs Brown', *The Hogarth Essays* no. 1, Hogarth Press, London, 1924.

Woolf, V., 'The Cinema', 1926, Woolf Online, www.woolfonline.com/timepasses/?q=essays/cinema/full (accessed 6 October 2016).

Yarnold, E., 'D'Arcy, Martin Cyril (1888–1976)', *Oxford Dictionary of National Biography*, Oxford University Press, Oxford, 2004; online edn, January 2011, www.oxforddnb.com/view/article/30998 (accessed 18 October 2016).

AUDIOVISUAL RESOURCES

Bragg, M. (presenter), with A. Pasternak Slater, D. Bradshaw and J. Bowen, 'Decline and Fall', *In Our Time*, BBC Radio 4, first broadcast 21 February 2013, www.bbc.co.uk/programmes/b01qmbsc (accessed 21 October 2016).

Granger, D., Interview in the 2011 DVD release of *Brideshead Revisited*, directed by C. Sturridge and M. Lindsay-Hogg, Acorn Media (Granada 1981).

Greenidge, T. (director), *The Scarlet Woman*, film, 1924, written by E. Waugh, http://player.bfi. org.uk/film/watch-the-scarlet-woman-1924 (accessed 3 October 2016).

Jarrold, J. (director), *Brideshead Revisited*, BBC Films, 2008.

Manley, J. 'Guy's Deleted Nippers: War Trilogy Variant Endings Persist and Proliferate', paper at 'Evelyn Waugh and His Circle' international conference, Leicester, 2015, https://soundcloud. com/artshumlaw/martin-stannard-donat-gallagher-jeff-manley-textual-editing-panel (accessed 26 October 2016).

Robertson, T.W., *School*, play, premiered at the Prince of Wales Theatre, London, 1869.

Scherfig, L. (director), *The Riot Club*, film, Blueprint Pictures, 2014.

Wade, L. *Posh*, play, premiered at the Royal Court Theatre, London, 2010.

Image Credits

Illustrations on pp. 77–140 © Amy Dodd.

xv, xviii, 4, 7, 11, 13, 14, 16, 17, 19, 20, 21, 22, 23 Courtesy Alexander Waugh.
29 Courtesy British Film Institute.
53r London, British Library, Add MS. 81057/© British Library/Bridgeman Images.
25 Oxford, Bodleian Library, *Isis*, 7 March 1923, Per. G.A. Oxon. 4° 145.
39 Oxford, Bodleian Library, *Cherwell*, 2 February 1924, Per. G.A. Oxon 4° 448.
40 Oxford, Bodleian Library, *Isis*, 24 January 1923, Per. G.A. Oxon 4° 145.
44 Oxford, Bodleian Library, *Cherwell*, 1 August 1923, Per. G.A. Oxon 4° 448.
32 Oxford, Bodleian Library, 254399 e.464.
36 Oxford, Bodleian Library, *Isis*, 24 May 1923, Per. G.A. Oxon 4° 145.
37 Oxford, Bodleian Library, Cary C 748.
56 Oxford, Bodleian Library, MS. Eng. c. 7256, fols 83–115.
71 © Entertainment Pictures/Alamy.
3 Harry Ransom Center, The University of Austin at Texas, Evelyn Waugh Collection 8.5.
33 Harry Ransom Center, The University of Austin at Texas, Evelyn Waugh Collection, 3.2.
34 Harry Ransom Center, The University of Austin at Texas, Evelyn Waugh Collection, 3.10.
35l Harry Ransom Center, The University of Austin at Texas, Evelyn Waugh book collection
    call no. AP 4 Y4 WAU.
47 Harry Ransom Center, The University of Austin at Texas, Evelyn Waugh Collection, 1.7,
    p. 92.
68 With the permission of the Principal, Fellows and Scholars of Hertford College in the
    University of Oxford.
5 Courtesy Lancing College Archive.
2 Leeds University Library, Fay and Geoffrey Elliot Collection.
28 Leeds University Library, Fay and Geoffrey Elliot Collection; courtesy Royal Institution of
    Cornwall.
30l Courtesy Martin Stannard.
75 Wikimedia Commons.
26, 30r, 35r, 38, 53l, 61, 67, 72 Private collection.

Index

Acton, Daphne 132
Acton, Harold 9, 12, 23, 25, 26, 27–9, 38, 54, 86, 127–9, 134
Aesthetes 27–8, 97, 134
Arnold, Matthew 104
Asquith, Katharine 61

Balfour, John Patrick Douglas, 3rd Baron Kinross 97
Bandaranaike, S.W.R.D. 7, 110–12
Beardsley, Aubrey 34–5, 37
Betjeman, John 55
Boothby, Robert 23
Boyle, Stuart 36, 37
Byrne, Paula 51, 69
Burne-Jones, Edward 135

Cameron, David 71
Campion, Edmund 114–17, 130
Carew, Dudley 6
Carroll, Lewis (Revd Charles Lutwidge Dodgson) 75, 107–8
    Alice in Wonderland 108
    Through the Looking Glass 107–8
Charles I, King 133
Cherwell magazine 29, 35, 39, 44, 55, 73, 104
Churchill, Randolph 18
Clifford Bax, The Golden Hind 39
Cockburn, Claud 9
Compton Mackenzie, Sinister Street 4–5
Connolly, Cyril 23, 128
Cooper, Diana 80, 131
Counsell, Dr Herbert ('Doggins') 85, 128

Cruttwell, C.R.M.F. 8, 40–41, 42, 98–9, 100–102
Danvers, Henry, first Earl of Danby 138
Dickens, Charles 90
Dodgson, Charles see Lewis Carroll 107
Driberg, Tom 9, 92–5
    Ruling Passions 93
Duggan, Alfred 12, 97, 124
Dulac, Edmund 34–5, 37
D'Arcy, Father Martin Cyril 59, 115

Eimerl, Sarel 60
Eliot, T.S., The Waste Land 28
Elizabeth I, Queen 85, 114

Fitzherbert, Giles 23
Fleming, Jean and Philla 3
Freeman, John 59
Frideswide, Saint 133
Fulford, Roger 6

Gardiner, Gerald 41
Gardner, Evelyn (1st wife) 11–12, 14, 116, 141
Gill, Eric 35, 38
Glen, Alexander ('Sandy') 141–2
Graham, Alastair 9–10, 12, 30, 53–4, 63, 74, 94, 122–3, 129, 140, 142
Green, Henry 73
Greene, Graham 97
Greenidge, Terence 8–9, 23–4, 29, 82, 98, 100, 128
    The Scarlet Woman 29, 82–3, 98
Guinness, Desmond 23

Haile Selassie, Emperor 111
Harrod, Dominick 23
Harrod, Henry 23
Harrod, Roy 23
Hastings, Selina 43, 50, 93
Heath Mount School 2
Heckstall-Smith, Hugh 95
Herbert, Laura *see* Waugh
Hodges, Lucy (nanny) 1, 2
Hollis, Christopher 97–9, 104, 110–11
Howard, Brian 134
Howard, William, Lord Clonmore 99

Isham, Gyles 82
Isis magazine 24, 29, 31, 36, 37, 40, 41, 43

Jackson, Sir Thomas 79
Johnson, Boris 71
Jungman, Teresa ('Baby') 12

Kermode, Frank 72
Knox, Father Ronald 130–32

Lancing College 5, 6, 7, 8, 9, 24, 32, 34, 40, 42, 52, 92
   Corpse Club 6
   Lancing College Magazine 6
Laycock, Lieutenant-Colonel Robert 16–17
Liddell, Henry 107
Linnaeus, Carl 138–9
London Mercury 39
Lygon, Hugh 12, 27, 140–42
Lygon, Maimie 141–2

MacCarthy, Desmond 51–2
McDonnell, Randal, 8th Earl of Antrim 23
Machin, Philip 8
Malory, Thomas, *Morte D'Arthur* 4
Mendl, Charles 19
Milthorpe, Naomi 112
Mitford, Nancy 20, 116, 131
Molson, Hugh, later Baron Molson 6–7, 42, 54, 100
Murray, Basil 129

Oxford
   Alice's Shop 107–9, 130
   Balliol College 82, 96–9
   Botanic Garden 136–9
   Bullingdon Club 69, 71
   Campion Hall 114–17
   Canal 103–6
   The Chequers 121, 122
   Christ Church 80, 107, 110, 133–5
   Druid's Head 122
   Hall Brothers 85–8
   Hertford College 7, 27, 50, 68, 78–80, 89, 96, 97, 100, 101
   Holywell Music Room 82
   Hypocrites Club 9, 63, 92–5, 97
   The Junk Shop 100–102
   Maltby's the Bookbinders 118–20
   Merton Street 140–42
   Nag's Head 122
   New College 88–91
   New Reform Club 128
   New Theatre 81–4
   Old Palace 130–32
   Old Sheep Shop *see* Alice's Shop
   Oxford Union 7, 8, 40, 44, 55, 56, 110–13, 122
   Railway Station 127–9
   St John's College 114–17
   The Turf 122
   White Rose Club 128
Oxford Broom journal 29, 38–9
Oxford Fortnightly Review 29, 40
Oxford University Dramatic Society (OUDS) 30, 43, 81–2, 88

Pares, Richard 7, 9, 42, 43, 97–9, 104, 129, 140
The Pistol Troop Magazine 2–4
Plunket Greene, Olivia 11, 123
Ponsonby, Matthew, 2nd Baron Ponsonby of Shulbrede 54
Powell, Anthony 10, 61, 63–4, 98
   Dance to the Music of Time 63–4
Pritchett, V.S. 57

Quennell, Peter 9, 48, 128
Quiller Couch, Arthur 67

The Rhesus 30, 88
Riot Club, film 71
Railway Club 23, 85, 127–9
Roberts, Sydney 128
Rodd, Peter 129
Rossetti, Dante Gabriel 11, 68

Rowse, A.L. 9, 27–9, 124, 134, 140–41
Russell, Conrad 80

Sheppard, Anderson 86
Sissons, Harold 104
Sitwell, Edith 28, 41
Sitwell, Osbert 28
Sparrow, John 23, 120
The Spectator 58
Sutro, John 23, 44, 55–6, 104, 128–9
Sykes, Christopher 17, 23

Tandy, Arthur 31
Thynne, Henry, 6th Marquess of Bath 23

Urquhart, Francis Fortescue ('Sligger') 9, 43, 97–9

Waugh, Alec (brother) 1, 2, 3, 4, 6, 13, 16, 67, 82, 86, 89, 100, 141
    The Loom of Youth 6
Waugh, Arthur (father) 1–5, 10, 15, 16, 34, 81–84, 88–91, 115
    Julius Seesawcer, Or, A Storm in a Tea-cup 82
Waugh, Auberon (son) 15, 17, 18, 23
Waugh, Evelyn Arthur St John
    Combe Florey home 22, 24
    childhood 1–7
    conversion to Catholicism 12, 115–17, 125–6, 138
    death 24
    marriage to Evelyn Gardner 9, 11–12, 14, 116, 141
    marriage to Laura Herbert 14–15, 115–17
    Piers Court home 15
    Underhill family home 1–4, 83–4, 90
    see also Aesthetes, Hertford College, Heath Mount School, Lancing College, Waugh works
Waugh, Evelyn, works
    'Anthony, Who Sought Things That Were Lost' 42–3
    Basil Seal Rides Again 129
    Black Mischief 31, 46, 101, 111, 112, 120, 141
    Brideshead Revisited 18–19, 28, 46–59, 63, 69, 71, 79–80, 83, 89–90, 94, 108, 122–4, 131, 134–6, 141–2
    'The Balance' 64–6, 69, 74, 86, 105
    'Converted to Rome: Why It Has Happened to Me' 126

Decline and Fall 10, 31–2, 60–61, 66–75, 101
Edmund Campion: Jesuit and Martyr 115–17, 132
'Edward of Unique Achievement' 42 , 70, 105
Hamlet review 40, 43–4
A Handful of Dust 14, 89–90
Helena 19, 21, 131
The Life of the Right Reverend Ronald Knox 132
A Little Learning, 8, 23–4, 29, 32, 39, 46, 48, 52–4, 57–63, 67, 70, 74, 79, 83, 85, 93–5, 97, 99, 101, 111–12, 119, 122–4, 137
Love Among the Ruins 21, 32
The Loved One 20, 36, 37
Men at Arms 21, 131
Officers and Gentlemen 21, 120
'Out of Depth' 138
The Ordeal of Gilbert Pinfold 23, 55, 87
'Portrait of Young Man with Career' 42
P.R.B.: An Essay on the Pre-Raphaelite Brotherhood, 1847–1854 10
Put Out More Flags 15, 16, 46, 124–5, 137
Rossetti: His Life and Works 10–11, 67–8
Scoop! 15, 101, 120
Scott-King's Modern Europe 20
Sword of Honour trilogy 21, 89, 91, 120, 131–2; see also Men at Arms, Officers and Gentlemen, Unconditional Surrender
Unconditional Surrender 21, 119–20
Vile Bodies 12, 32, 46, 66, 83, 108–9
Work Suspended 91
Waugh, Harriet (daughter) 17, 18
Waugh, James (son) 17, 22
Waugh, Laura, née Herbert (2nd wife) 14–22, 115–17
Waugh, Mary (daughter) 15
Waugh, Meg (daughter) 17, 18, 21
Waugh, Septimus (son) 20, 22
Waugh, Teresa (daughter) 15, 17, 18
Wolsey, Cardinal Thomas 133
Wong, Anna May 19
Woolf, Leonard 67
Woolf, Virginia 41–2

Yorke, Henry see Henry Green

Young, Dick 60, 72
The Yellow Book 34–5

Walton St.

Junk Shop

St. John's College

Beaumont St.

St Giles

New Theatre

Balliol College

STATION
½ MILE

George St.

Broad Street

Railway Station

Oxford Union

Chequers

High Stree

St Michael'st

Canal

Alice's Shop

Eat Me

Christ Church

St Alda

Hypocrites' Club

The Old Palace